SERVICE-ORIENTED ARCHITECTURE
SOA Strategy, Methodology, and Technology

OTHER AUERBACH PUBLICATIONS

Agent-Based Manufacturing and Control Systems: New Agile Manufacturing Solutions for Achieving Peak Performance
Massimo Paolucci and Roberto Sacile
ISBN: 1574443364

Curing the Patch Management Headache
Felicia M. Nicastro
ISBN: 0849328543

Cyber Crime Investigator's Field Guide, Second Edition
Bruce Middleton
ISBN: 0849327687

Disassembly Modeling for Assembly, Maintenance, Reuse and Recycling
A. J. D. Lambert and Surendra M. Gupta
ISBN: 1574443348

The Ethical Hack: A Framework for Business Value Penetration Testing
James S. Tiller
ISBN: 084931609X

Fundamentals of DSL Technology
Philip Golden, Herve Dedieu,
and Krista Jacobsen
ISBN: 0849319137

The HIPAA Program Reference Handbook
Ross Leo
ISBN: 0849322111

Implementing the IT Balanced Scorecard: Aligning IT with Corporate Strategy
Jessica Keyes
ISBN: 0849326214

Information Security Fundamentals
Thomas R. Peltier, Justin Peltier,
and John A. Blackley
ISBN: 0849319579

Information Security Management Handbook, Fifth Edition, Volume 2
Harold F. Tipton and Micki Krause
ISBN: 0849332109

Introduction to Management of Reverse Logistics and Closed Loop Supply Chain Processes
Donald F. Blumberg
ISBN: 1574443607

Maximizing ROI on Software Development
Vijay Sikka
ISBN: 0849323126

Mobile Computing Handbook
Imad Mahgoub and Mohammad Ilyas
ISBN: 0849319714

MPLS for Metropolitan Area Networks
Nam-Kee Tan
ISBN: 084932212X

Multimedia Security Handbook
Borko Furht and Darko Kirovski
ISBN: 0849327733

Network Design: Management and Technical Perspectives, Second Edition
Teresa C. Piliouras
ISBN: 0849316081

Network Security Technologies, Second Edition
Kwok T. Fung
ISBN: 0849330270

Outsourcing Software Development Offshore: Making It Work
Tandy Gold
ISBN: 0849319439

Quality Management Systems: A Handbook for Product Development Organizations
Vivek Nanda
ISBN: 1574443526

A Practical Guide to Security Assessments
Sudhanshu Kairab
ISBN: 0849317061

The Real-Time Enterprise
Dimitris N. Chorafas
ISBN: 0849327776

Software Testing and Continuous Quality Improvement, Second Edition
William E. Lewis
ISBN: 0849325242

Supply Chain Architecture: A Blueprint for Networking the Flow of Material, Information, and Cash
William T. Walker
ISBN: 1574443577

The Windows Serial Port Programming Handbook
Ying Bai
ISBN: 0849322138

SERVICE-ORIENTED ARCHITECTURE
SOA Strategy, Methodology, and Technology

James P. Lawler

H. Howell-Barber

CRC Press
Taylor & Francis Group
Boca Raton London New York

CRC Press is an imprint of the
Taylor & Francis Group, an **informa** business

AN AUERBACH BOOK

CRC Press
Taylor & Francis Group
6000 Broken Sound Parkway NW, Suite 300
Boca Raton, FL 33487-2742

First issued in paperback 2019

© 2008 by Taylor & Francis Group, LLC
CRC Press is an imprint of Taylor & Francis Group, an Informa business

No claim to original U.S. Government works

ISBN-13: 978-1-4200-4500-0 (hbk)
ISBN-13: 978-0-367-38823-2 (pbk)

Library of Congress Cataloging-in-Publication Data

Lawler, James (James P.)
  Service-oriented architecture : SOA strategy, methodology, and technology / James Lawler and H. Howell-Barber.
     p. cm.
  Includes bibliographical references and index.
  ISBN 978-1-4200-4500-0 (alk. paper)
  1. Business enterprises--Computer networks--Management. 2. Information technology--Management. 3. Web services. 4. Computer network architectures. I. Howell-Barber, H. II. Title.

HD30.2.L395 2008
658'.05--dc22   2007015612

Visit the Taylor & Francis Web site at
http://www.taylorandfrancis.com

and the CRC Press Web site at
http://www.crcpress.com

Dedication

For my parents, Matthew J. Lawler and Ann McCartin

James P. Lawler

For my daughter and leading-edge technical advisor, Cynthia Barber-Mingo

H. Howell-Barber

Contents

SECTION 1: SERVICE-ORIENTED ARCHITECTURE (SOA) STRATEGY

SECTION 2: SERVICE-ORIENTED ARCHITECTURE (SOA) METHODOLOGY

SECTION 3: SERVICE-ORIENTED ARCHITECTURE (SOA) TECHNOLOGY

Foreword

Service-oriented architecture (SOA), which applies loosely coupled and interoperable software services to support business processes of firms, furnishes a mechanism for defining business models. SOA can help ensure that services accurately represent those business models. Based on several years of research and field studies, *Service-Oriented Architecture: Strategy, Methodology, and Technology* is a book that will help business practitioners who are involved in adopting and deploying SOA to understand and use SOA successfully.

This book presents a distinctive technology-agnostic program management methodology that uses an iterative approach to develop service-oriented solutions. Focused on business readers but highly useful to technical readers who must interface with business staff, the book clarifies in a technology-neutral manner how the success of implementing SOA depends more on business factors than on technical ones. *Service-Oriented Architecture: Strategy, Methodology, and Technology* contributes to the literature of best business practices and is a "must-read" for business professionals involved in SOA.

A unique feature of this book is the inclusion of 15 case studies. Each study is based on an actual business SOA strategy. The studies originate from diverse economic sectors, including non-profit. The authors evaluate the practices and the strategies of SOA in these firms and organizations and *post facto* apply their program management methodology to them. The inclusion of "lessons learned" for each of the case studies provides invaluable information and insight into the proper usage of SOA.

James P. Lawler and H. Howell-Barber have more than 65 combined years of experience in business process, information management, and project and program management methodology, and they have published numerous studies on business strategy and technology.

This new book, *Service-Oriented Architecture: Strategy, Methodology, and Technology*, will make a significant impact on both the theory and practice of SOA.

John C. Molluzzo
Chair of Information Systems Department
Ivan G. Seidenberg School of Computer Science and Information Systems
Pace University, New York City

Acknowledgments

This book would not have been possible without the cooperation of business and technical managers as needed in the business firms in the case studies and without the fundamental initiatives of these firms in investing in a service-oriented architecture (SOA) strategy.

We want to thank Lisa Smith, Managing Editor, Research, *Information Week*, for her cooperation in permitting us to include figures from *Information Week* in the strategy section of the book.

We want to thank Dr. Susan M. Merritt, Dean of the Ivan G. Seidenberg School of Computer Science and Information Systems of Pace University, in New York City, for enabling Dr. Lawler to complete this book under a flexible teaching schedule in 2007.

We want to thank our colleagues, Jonathan Hill, Assistant Dean of the Seidenberg School and a co-author with us of an analysis of Web services in 2004; Dr. James W. Gabberty, an associate professor in the school; and also Levsiri Munasinghe, of the Royal Bank of Canada, who contributed ideas that improved the final draft of the book immeasurably.

We also want to thank Alina Joshi and Bhaskar Sahrawat, graduate students of Pace University, for their help in researching the descriptive information on firms in the case studies in the methodology section of the book.

Finally, we want to thank our editor, John Wyzalek of Auerbach Publications, for his encouragement and support.

About the Authors

James P. Lawler, D.P.S., is an associate professor of information systems in the Ivan G. Seidenberg School of Computer Science and Information Systems at Pace University in New York City. He graduated with a doctorate in computing studies from Pace University.

His extensive experience of more than 30 years is in business information strategies in industry. Dr. Lawler is a published author on topics including customer relationship management (CRM), E-commerce, and Web services, and has been the principal author of an analysis of services strategy in 2004. This paper was awarded the *best paper* of the Information Systems Education Conference (ISECON) that year. More recently, he again achieved notice with the award for *best paper* of the INFORMS (Institute for Operations Research and the Management Sciences) Conference in 2007. He presented a paper on *Methodology for Educating Information Systems Students on the New Paradigm of Service-Oriented Architecture*, which is based on generic principles of this book.

He can be contacted at jlawler@pace.edu.

H. Howell-Barber is founder and president of HBiNK, LLC, in New York. She has extensive experience of more than 35 years in business process management and program and project management methodologies in industry. Ms. Barber has held directorships of technology in the financial services industry and is currently a consultant on business process management systems, customized service-oriented methodology, and services technologies and tools. She is a published author of analyses of services in 2004 and 2006. She graduated from Brooklyn College in New York. She can be contacted at h.howell@verizon.net.

SERVICE-ORIENTED ARCHITECTURE (SOA) STRATEGY

1

The journey of a thousand miles begins with a single step.

—Old Chinese Proverb

Chapter 1

Introduction to Strategy

The background of this book on service-oriented architecture (SOA) is based on an earlier analysis of business automation and Web services begun by an information systems graduate student in 2003 in a *Web services: processes and technologies* independent project program, in the Ivan G. Seidenberg School of Computer Science and Information Systems, at Pace University.

A final analysis of Web services was completed by us in 2004, in collaboration with business colleagues at firms in industry and with academic researchers at the university.[1] This analysis was conducted of firms in the financial industry, which was considered by practitioner reputation and by us as aggressive in the adoption of services technology at that time. We analyzed the specific experiences of the financial firms and the generic findings of consulting and service technology firms in services strategy. That analysis focused on 36 business factors, methodological factors, and technical factors in the design, development, and implementation of a services strategy. Examples of business factors in the firms included business client contribution to executive sponsorship. Methodological factors included culture of innovation to life-cycle project management, and technical factors included executive technology leadership to integration of platform technology firms (vendors). All factors in the analysis were construed as critical in an effective services strategy.

Results from four case studies and literature surveys of fourteen firms in the analysis in 2004 were that financial firms that led projects in services with business factors — especially business benefit driver, customer demand, and focus on process integration — had more success with Web services than firms in this industry that led with the functionality of platform technology. Business strategy defined by business departments in the firms, not technology, was considered crucial in a Web services strategy. These results, presented at conferences in 2004 and published in

3

2005, were beneficial for firms in the financial industry, and in nonfinancial industries that were considering an approach to application automation and information architecture founded on Web services.

Since the completion of the analysis of Web services in the financial industry, we continued the research of services into 2005, 2006, and 2007, as SOA was and is being adopted by financial firms on actual automation applications. The best of the adoptions appears, as in Web services, to be based on business considerations, not on applications and technology. Consulting firms disclose constant adoption if not complete deployment of SOA projects in industry.[2] Gartner Inc. forecasts that 80 percent of development will be based on an SOA model by 2008.[3] Despite a current absence of financial and nonfinancial firms completing a composite of all processes of a business as services, composed in *a fully deployed SOA* in a service-oriented enterprise (SOE) idealized by consultants, firms in the software technology industry continue to develop and extend service solutions as tactics in an assumed strategy. SOA is not considered a fad but a development as consequential to industry as the Internet.[4]

If in doubt, the potential of services and services technology is forecast by Bill Gates to dwarf the Internet![5]

Because of the commotion and the hype on services technology, we decided to expand our studies to SOA from financial firms to SOA in nonfinancial industries. Further study is appropriate, as business firms are beginning to achieve the benefits of business and technical agility and flexibility in business processes. They are deploying Web services in *bona fide* collections of business processes coupled loosely in *business domains* (e.g., features of software in processing a customer inquiry). Each of the services constitutes business functionality that can be brought together to facilitate a business process. Firms are concurrently deploying technical services or *technical domains* (e.g., data integration and data warehousing), although the focus of this book is business process services.

None of the business domains indicated above were apparent during our 2004 study. SOA, as applications exposing functionality and information as services accessible by different business client or "consumer" departments in a firm, is a concept currently defined extensively in the literature of technology practitioners. The distinction of SOA, in contrast to earlier hyped technologies, is in the actual benefits that firms are now achieving. Business managers in industry can clearly comprehend the benefits. Agility, efficiency and flexibility of business processes are achievable as goals of information technology (IT) departments.[6]

Business Process Management (BPM)

To achieve the goals of services, SOA is converging with business process management (BPM) in business firms in which managers are conscious of the criticality of business processes.

BPM is an approach for achieving business goals, coordinating the end-to-end processes of firms, establishing best practices, and furnishing software, such as in a business process management system (BPMS), to describe, analyze, and enhance the efficiency of the processes against business goals. A BPMS helps in graphically modeling processes with Web Services Business Process Execution Language (WS-BPEL) in a manner such that the IT department can implement or improve functions of the processes. Business processes consist of a set of logically related tasks designed to achieve defined business outcomes,[7] such as compliance, engineering, finance, human resources, logistics, manufacturing, marketing, sales, service, or supply of a product.

BPM consists of the business process logic apart from the code of the applications behind the processes, which helps in improving the processes if BPM is actually a consumer of services in an SOA.

One can consider the BPM as a base for a business-oriented architecture. From this base, BPM contributes to the betterment and flexibility of competitive processes, enabled by information technology in improving the processes.[8] Convergence of SOA with BPM affords benefits in combining services as processes, facilitating faster changes "on demand" to processes as services, and integrating processes as services in firms. *SOA with BPM can competitively differentiate the performance of enterprise processes of firms* in a continuous improvement strategy or a differentiation strategy[9] by driving greater productivity and by solving business problems. Figure 1.1 conceptualizes BPM and SOA.

Firms may choose a business-centric modeling method or alternatively a data modeling method in analyzing the efficiency of processes.

Benefits of improving business processes, enhancing customer experiences, enabling improved partner firm relationships, or improving the time-to-market of new processes or products in an eventual deployment of services are discerned by firms investing in SOA. Business methods combined with an SOA strategy may enable firms to respond faster to frequent opportunities and threats in their industries. Benefits in cost savings on software development are forecast to be greater than an aggregate $50 billion in firms globally for 2006 to 2010.[10] The bulk of the savings in software derives from eventual elimination of enterprise application integration (EAI), middleware and point-to-point proprietary solutions, and a gradual reduction in redundancy of software coding, due to reusability of services in an SOA throughout firms.

Figure 1.2 depicts the benefits and goals of an SOA.

Firms are investing in services technology because of the benefits. Figure 1.3 depicts investment in 2006 in SOA.

Although costs exceed savings in the beginning of an SOA, savings are forecast to exceed the costs of a fully deployed SOA.

Approximately 50 percent of firms cite a return on investment (ROI) in the first 12 months of deployment.[11]

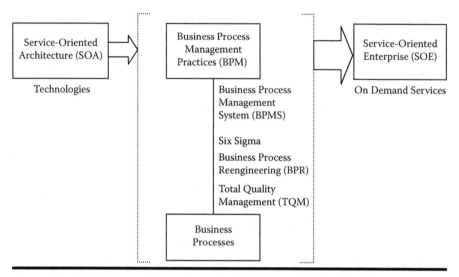

Figure 1.1   Business process management (BPM) and SOA.

Enterprise Architecture

Deployment of an SOA is based on a strategy founded on the business objectives of firms.

Fundamental to the foundation is a business model that consists of the business objectives and the business strategy of the firms and the core processes to achieve the objectives of the strategy. *Business enterprise architecture defines the design of detailed tasks of the business processes, the business policies* (e.g., management of metadata), *and the information technologies included in an IT infrastructure, based on the definition of what the firm does as a business.* This infrastructure includes the integration of applications, databases, information, standards, and platform technologies behind the processes. An SOA includes the bulk of enterprise architecture.

Nevertheless, the enterprise architecture of services is based on business decisions or a definition of business strategy, and not on technical decisions or technology strategy. Infrastructure architecture deals with the bulk of technical decisions. Technology is secondary to business in an SOA. Figure 1.4 depicts business-driven enterprise architecture in an SOA strategy.

Important to the foundation is business process planning and orientation of the technologies to services, as enterprise architecture is a key enabler for business flexibility and the integration of processes, services, and technologies in firms. Governance models, which are discussed later in this section, ensure that IT projects conform to enterprise architecture, but an SOA governance model ensures conformance of projects on services to the enterprise architecture in an SOA strategy that leads to an SOE. An evolving SOA includes frameworks for coordinating the

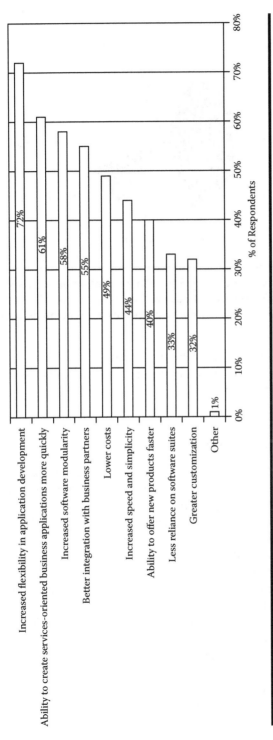

Figure 1.2 Benefits and goals of an SOA. (*Source: Information Week* Research SOA/Web Services Survey of 273 business technology professionals in 200 firms using SOA/Web Services [Multiple Responses], September 2006. With permission.)

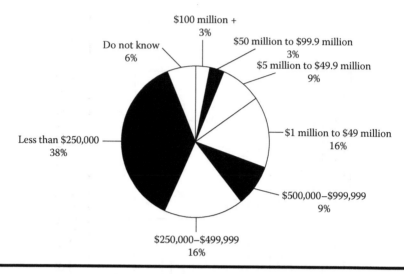

Figure 1.3   Investment in 2006 in SOA. (*Source: Information Week* Research SOA/Web Services Survey of 273 business technology professionals in 200 firms using SOA/Web Services [Multiple Responses], September 2006. With permission.)

technical and business decisions of diverse constituencies in a firm. Governance, IT infrastructure, enterprise architecture, and business modeling are the foundation for the benefits of an SOA in firms.

SOA and Web Services

The benefits of an SOA are the dominant hype of the literature on services technology in 2007 — not Web services, but an analysis of SOA is not adequate without defining from the literature Web services in contrast to SOA.

SOA is defined as "[an enabling] framework for integrating business processes and supporting information technology infrastructure as [loosely coupled and] secure, standardized components — services — that can be reused and combined to address changing business priorities."[12]

Web services are defined as "a family of technologies that consist of specifications, protocols, and industry-based standards that are used by heterogeneous applications to communicate, collaborate, and exchange information among themselves in a secure, reliable, and interoperable manner."[13] Services in an SOA are modules of business or technical functionality with exposed interfaces to the functionality. Web services are the organizing principles of SOA at this time.

Services can perform a discrete function (i.e., atomic Web services or component SOA services) or a number of functions (i.e., composite services).

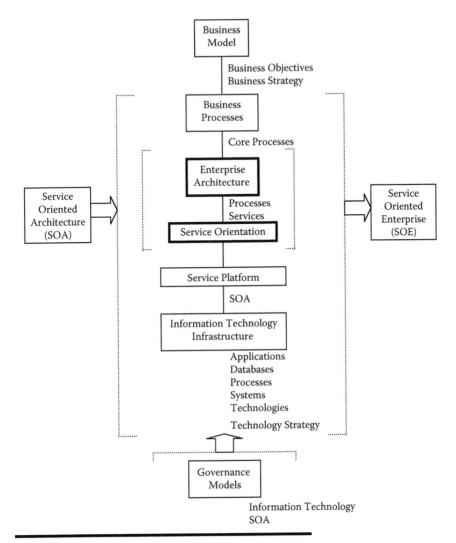

Figure 1.4 Enterprise architecture in an SOA strategy.

An SOA is deployed on a platform of Web services,[14] Web services standards, and recommendations from .NET and Java. Simple Object Access Protocol (SOAP)* is an Extensible Markup Language- (XML) based protocol for exchanging messages between interacting services. Web Services Description Language (WSDL) is an XML standard for describing the services, the location of the services, and the invocation methods of the services; and Universal Description, Discovery, and

---

* SOAP can be impacted by Representational State Transfer (REST) in the simplification of Web services, but REST was new in the period of our study and thus not reviewed by us.

Integration (UDDI) is the standard for publishing the services in a registry that can be discovered by applications on any computing platform. SOA is primarily founded on Web services standards, which is important in the interoperability of an SOA with non-proprietary software technologies. An SOA can, nevertheless, be deployed on other technologies.

In short, an SOA may be considered a framework for practices that effectively apply Web services. Web services integrate into an SOA and enable enterprise integration of services throughout a firm.

Strategy of an SOA

In a business strategy, Web services automate applications in departmental, limited, and localized if not smaller solutions, which are purely tactical to business firms. Because of shorter deployment efforts, the benefits of Web services are currently more tangible than those of an SOA. Because of longer deployment efforts and the functional complexity of an SOA, benefits may not be immediately tangible as in Web services. In contrast to Web services, an SOA automates processes in business units if not larger business unit-to-business unit or firm-to-firm solutions, which are strategic to firms. An SOA is deployed on a path leading to an SOE, which is idealized in the technology industry as significantly strategic to firms.

Figure 1.5 depicts an optimal theory of deployment of services from Web services to an SOA, which may not be sequential as depicted in the figure because the reality of the deployment of the services may be nonsequential.

In this book, the business context of the benefits of deploying services technology is more in the differentiating strategic SOA solutions than in the tactical Web services solutions.

The challenge in analyzing an SOA is that benefits are not competitively differentiating enterprise processes in most of the firms deploying an SOA.

Benefits described previously and in Figure 1.2 are achievable in firms beginning to deploy services, and are encouraging to us, as they may be tangible in impact, but they are still *tactical* to firms, as with the deployment of Web services. Firms are continuing to evolve incremental solutions of services with an SOA. Evolution may be from basic data and logic services, functional intermediary services, and encapsulated knowledge process services internal to business departments and business units of firms to enterprise integration services external to firms.[15] The goal of firms investing in an SOA is an SOE allowing further integration of current "what-is" processes and future "what-if" processes throughout the firms.

Benefits of an SOE lie effectively in the flexibility in changing business enterprise processes of the firm as the business models of the firms change due to competitor conditions, customer demands, or global pressures. Business models may also

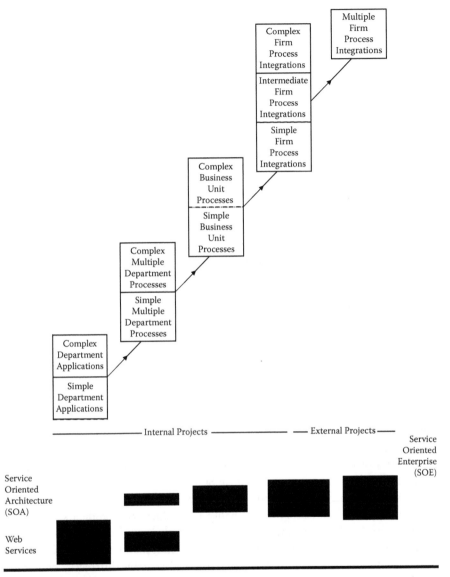

Figure 1.5 Deployment of services from Web services to SOA. *Note:* Density of the lower shading in figure is depicting the decreased deployment of Web services and the increased deployment of SOA from the beginning of SOA to the actualization of SOE.

change due to regulatory needs (e.g., the Gramm-Leach-Bliley Financial Services Modernization Act of 1999, the Health Insurance Portability and Accountability Act [HIPAA] of 1996, the Sarbanes-Oxley [SOX] Act of 2002, the Securities

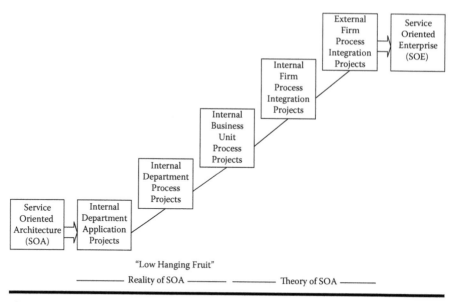

Figure 1.6   Evolution of an SOA.

Exchange Commission (SEC) Rule 17a-14, and the USA Patriot Act). These needs frequently drive the implementation of an SOA. Benefits of an SOE lie in mixing and matching services in other "on-demand" solutions.

Figure 1.6 depicts an optimal theory of the evolution of an SOA, which may not be sequential as depicted because the reality of the evolution of an SOA may be nonsequential.

Benefits of further business agility, efficient and flexible processes, and future integrated applications from an SOA in an SOE can differentiate the business model of firms in customer value propositions and are *strategic* to the firms. Such benefits can contribute *unique* feature functionality in products and product services that can be appreciated by customers and that can be perceived by them as better than or different from the products of competitors.[16] The benefits of an SOA, if not an SOE, can differentiate firms for those that desire discernable differentiation in their industry, but there are firms that may be content with merely continuous improvement or equivalency from services.

Differentiation of an SOA can be considered in *customer analytics* services for a customer care representative in contact with a potentially profitable or profitable customer, as described in the following examples.

Example of SOA as a Tactical Solution

Customer Care
Representative

Example of Customer Analytics Services

**Competitive Equivalency Strategy or
Continuous Improvement Strategy**

Customer

SOA can deliver information on all of the accounts, inquiries, and transactions of a profitable customer from different channels of interaction, such as mobile computing, telephone, or Web, and from diverse applications of business units and departments of a firm.

SOA can incrementally integrate the information into a Web-based desktop interface for the customer care representative.

The customer care representative, as a result, can have a 360-degree profile of the customer.

The representative can interact intelligently if the customer contacts the representative with a product inquiry over the telephone.

The customer expects an intelligent interaction with the representative on his inquiry.

The above deployment of an expected and good customer experience service is an example of a competitive equivalency strategy (i.e., the firm is equivalent in core services with competitor firms) or of continuous improvement strategy (i.e., the firm exceeds equivalency with competitor firms for a *definite* but short duration [e.g., three to six months]) from an SOA, but not of a competitive differentiation strategy (i.e., the firm exceeds equivalency with competitor firms for an *extended* and longer duration [e.g., one to two years]).

Example of SOA as a Strategic Solution

Customer Care
Representative

Example of Customer Analytics Services

Competitive Differentiation Strategy

Customer

SOA could deliver further information on customized products to market to this customer from marketing, sales and service analytic applications of the firm and from affiliated analytic databases of external partnered firms.

SOA could integrate the information into the desktop interface for the customer care representative.

The customer care representative, as a result, could have not only the 360-degree profile of this customer to interact intelligently, but also have knowledge of potential market basket scenarios to personalize products to this profitable customer beyond his initial product inquiry.

Further knowledge management functionality could be deployed on the desktop system for the representative, and a cost-saving self-service and search system on the Web could be deployed for the customer, for him to craft his own experience, from a library of services, without having the technology department create new applications.

The customer may not have expected a further intelligent interaction with the representative.

The above deployment of an unexpected and *great customer experience* service is an example of a *competitive differentiation strategy*, which can generate greater revenue and higher profit for firms sooner than on a continuous improvement strategy. The experience is of *composite service*s that are extensible and flexible, in integrating functionality and information from diverse applications into a common interface, in which the complexity and location of the information are transparent to the client. Firms can benefit highly by integrating Web-based technologies, such as an SOA, to acquire additional benefits from established systems.[17]

Figure 1.7 illustrates the benefits of competitive differentiation solutions in an SOA strategy.

An SOA in an SOE, however, is an idealized theory rather than a practice or a reality in 2007.[18]

To achieve the benefits of an SOA in a competitive differentiation strategy, technology managers and business managers in firms are confronted with a decision as to the best approach to deployment. Deploying to an SOA is more complex in concept than deploying to client/server technology from legacy technology or deploying to Web from client/server technology. Consideration of deployment of an SOA as a first mover, fast follower, or follower firm is difficult for managers.

Complexity in approaching an SOA as a project, as described in Figure 1.8, is clear in concerns of adopters. Figure 1.8 illustrates the importance of the complexity and the issues of services in deployment of an SOA strategy.

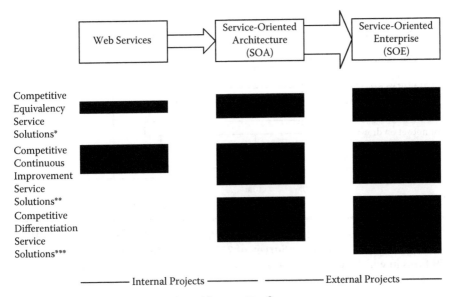

* Firm is equivalent in core services with competitor firms.
** Firm exceeds equivalency with competitor firms for a defined but short duration (e.g., 3–6 months).
*** Firm exceeds equivalency with competitor firms for an extended and longer duration (e.g., 1–2 years).

Figure 1.7 Competitive differentiation solutions in an SOA strategy. *Note:* Density of the shading in this figure is depicting a theory of increased deployment of services from competitive eqivalency to competitive differentiation service solutions.

Deployment, as depicted previously in Figure 1.6, appears to be examples more of "low hanging fruit" homogeneous internal departmental application projects, and less of internal business unit and external potentially invasive process projects, if not heterogeneous high-throughput, low-latency applications. Investment must not be on a simple pilot project, but on a complex strategy. Although departmental projects can be chosen for a few services that contribute faster impact or incremental ROI (return on investment), full return from an SOA is achieved on further projects, which are more complex and can be risky in contributing a return.

Investment in SOA projects on a path of an SOA strategy is difficult for firms, as the full savings exceed the full costs not at the beginning deployment of departmental projects but closer to the integration of business unit and external firm projects at full deployment. Such a strategy can be especially difficult for both small-sized and medium-sized firms, although they may not have the complex legacy integration requirements of large-sized firms. Investment in an SOA is a perpetual and risky strategy.

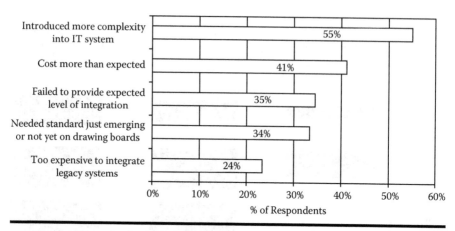

Figure 1.8 Issues in deployment of an SOA strategy. (*Source: Information Week* Research SOA/Web Services Survey of 273 business technology professionals in 49 firms in which SOA/Web Services fell below expectations [Multiple Responses], September 2006. With permission.)

Concerns may be from the current development of technology behind an SOA, if not the theory of SOA, that the reality of a shared SOE infrastructure may not be practical in a reasonable period. If an SOE is not practical in a short period, concerns may be in the evolution to a shared infrastructure.

Firms may be hesitant to adopt — if not deploy — an SOA due to the hype of the technology industry in frequently disparate platform solutions, specialty technologies, and standards of the technologies.

Hesitancy may stem from a culture where the technology department is not collaborative with business departments on technical solutions, not focused on business design or process integration,[19] or not knowledgeable in the methodology of object orientation and service orientation[20] on projects. The developmental methodology of an SOA is distinct from non-SOA methodologies, in that process and project requirements of different departments and business units for services in firms, in response to competitive conditions, customer demands or regulatory needs, are not fixed and frequently incomplete on pre- or post-deployed SOA projects. Non-SOA methodologies that include older "waterfall" models contradict enterprise demands of firms to be fast, flexible, incremental, innovative, and iterative in releases of services. Non-agile models are serial and slow in an SOA strategy.

Hesitancy may also stem from a lack of credibility in the knowledge of the IT department on the business strategy of firms.

Hesitancy can, moreover, derive from a history of ownership of processes by the business departments and of projects by the IT department, although the ownership of processes and projects of SOA is a joint program. Technical managers may have a formidable issue in not having business executive leadership on an SOA, as executive management may not be knowledgeable about SOA although technical executive sponsorship may be evident in the firms. IT staff may not be knowledgeable on the business nor perceived as partners with the business staff.

Hesitancies and concerns regarding SOA are analogous to earlier eras of innovation in software technologies, which advanced in adoption, analysis, design, development, and deployment stages. The issues of SOA, as discussed previously, are not in the simple and tactical application and departmental deployment stages, but rather on the path of complex business unit and enterprise process deployment stages that lead to an SOE in an SOA strategy. As the path begins with a defined process in departments and embraces more processes in more business units on more projects in parallel with other projects and with more and more technical and business staff, and as competitive conditions, customer demands, and regulatory scrutiny on the processes change concurrently for firms, control of the processes and the projects, and of the services technology, is critical in ensuring an evolving strategy.

Governance of Information Technology with an SOA Strategy

To address the concerns and hesitancies, control of processes and projects optimally begins at the beginning of deployment of the first services. Services are not controlled by a department or a business unit in firms but can be extended in firms and must be shared by departments and business units in the firms. Effective coordination of an SOA as the enterprise architecture demands governance of functionality of information technologies as services to a firm. Governance of service-oriented technology focuses on the following criteria:

- Core processes of the business model of the firm
- Changes to the processes that are critical to the competitive equivalency strategy, continuous improvement strategy, and competitive differentiation strategy of the firm, including opportunities in the processes for new systems and technologies
- Technology behind the services that can contribute to a competitive differentiation strategy and that can be piloted not only as software technology, but also as an SOA
- Plans to continue to be a leading-edge first mover or fast follower with services technology and to be a learning organization in educating the IT and business departments and business units on service orientation and SOA
- Responsibilities and roles of the IT department staff and business department and business unit staff in governance leadership in the proactive promotion of an SOA as a business strategy

Criteria on governance of service-oriented technology are enhanced and expanded from decisions on governance of technology[21] in an established IT engagement model.[22]

Effective governance controls the alignment of services to enterprise architecture of an SOA and the availability of services in firms, as an eventual SOE may create exception paths to services if required. From the beginning of projects, governance decides the priority of services for release throughout firms.

Governance is critical in achieving current and future agility, efficiency, and flexibility from core processes, projects, and technologies of firms investing in an SOA. It ensures consistency and interoperability among services, ensures the continuity of the benefits from services, evaluates technical and business metrics on the performance requirements and the reusability of services, and furnishes security to information exposed by services. It also ensures that technology strategy is synchronized with business strategy. It helps in controlling renegade services and may include incentives for development staff to reuse services.

Essentially, governance is critical in strategy.

Governance in firms investing in an SOA is a function that ideally reports to senior management. Governance requires an organization of business and technical staff,[23] including enterprise architectural planning and service development staff, which might control a catalog or a UDDI registry of services. Such a group or team may be formal or informal, although we advocate a formal organization for promotion of shared services in an SOA.

Governance may also require reorganization of technology and business departments and business units and staff into *business domains of services*, such as customer analytics in a previous example, which control the technology behind the services. Such reorganization can be a highly important issue for managers or staff in firms not cognizant of service orientation principles and reusability of services, but the business benefits of flexibility, efficiency, and agility of an SOA may not be maximized without it.

The complexity of an SOA creates a challenge in methodology for firms attempting to define an approach to the deployment of an SOA.

This book addresses the challenge.

Program Management Methodology

This book defines a practical program management methodology that can be complementary to project management methodologies already established in business firms. Dimensions of service orientation and an SOA are customizable in the project management methodologies by application of our program management methodology, by which processes can be identified with services. Methodologies in the firms are assumed to be agile approaches,[24] or characteristics of agile methods enhanced for control of complex systems, that are complimentary to our program management methodology. Earlier pre-Web project methods of non-agile systems development methodologies, requiring fixed procedural requirements, may not be appropriate for our program management methodology.

Our methodology assumes flexibility for changing process requirements of an SOA, because of external competitive conditions, customer demands, or regulatory needs or due to internal technical or business needs. It advocates delivery of frequent benefits and releases of services on an incremental and iterative project path that leads to an enterprise or full-firm SOE. It consists of frequent interaction of the technology department and the business departments and business units in the migration to a full SOE. It includes diversely skilled technical and business staff on smaller teams. This methodology is a hybrid approach, which is top-down in design from business management models and bottom-up in design from operations and platform technologies, and is appropriate for tactical and strategic SOA.

Figure 1.9 illustrates the approach of the program management methodology in this book.

The program management methodology in this book takes an agile approach to an SOA strategy that contributes the benefits of flexibility, efficiency, and agility to firms on the path to the idealized SOE.

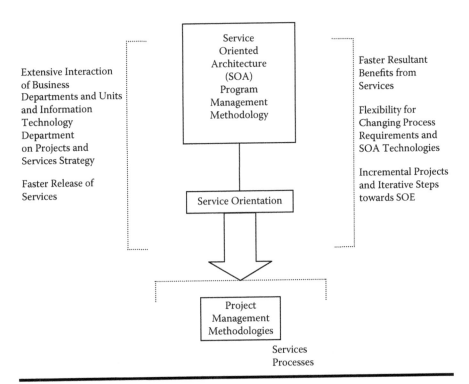

Figure 1.9 SOA program management methodology.

The aim of this book is to assist business managers and business staff, as well as technical program managers and project managers and staff, in comfortably adopting and deploying an SOA as a competitive differentiation strategy. Based on the authors' consulting experience in industry and research in services, in 2005 and 2006, one can define a comprehensive and disciplined *Methodology for Enabling Service-Oriented Architecture (MESOA)* program management methodology (see Section 2). This methodology comprises an integration of nine frameworks:

1. Framework of governance
2. Framework of communications
3. Framework of product realization
4. Framework of project management
5. Framework of architecture
6. Framework of data management
7. Framework of service management
8. Framework of human resource management
9. Framework of post implementation

Product realization in the above consists of analysis and design, development, deployment, and implementation stages. The frameworks consist of 57 business factors, procedural factors, and technical factors that can contribute to SOA as a successful strategy. Examples of business factors are competitive differential to process improvement focus. Procedural factors are information management to risk management. Technical factors are internal process domain to external SOA domain. These factors are expanded for SOA from 36 factors in our study of Web services in 2004 to ensure full *service orientation* of the frameworks.

The methodology in this book is distinct from established program management methodologies because it enables a controlled iterative phasing of projects in incremental steps in a definite service-oriented solution. This methodology is essentially an evolutionary version of non-agile and agile project management techniques that we distinguish in the customization of the techniques to SOA. Integrated in the methodology are the program responsibilities and roles of 62 corporate, business, governance, and technical staff, such as that of the executive sponsor, business analyst, enterprise architect, and integration specialist, whose roles are expanded on projects on the path of an SOA strategy.

This methodology is applied to commonly encountered practices in cases of 15 Fortune 10 to Fortune 1000 firms that are currently deploying the beginning of an SOA strategy. These are expanded from the four firms in the financial industry of the 2004 study and include automobile, banking, energy, health, insurance, manufacturing, technology, telecommunications, training, and travel in this book and new study. We applied our program management methodology *post facto* to the practices of the firms in 2005 and 2006, depicting frameworks and factors more enabling than other factors and frameworks in the SOA strategies of the firms. We evaluated the practices and strategies of SOA in these firms from generic industry literature and from specific interaction with technical and business project staff in a number of firms. We identified key state-of-the-art technologies of the SOA strategies in the firms. Because of competitive considerations of processes and of practices, we identify the firms anonymously in the book.

This book, and findings from our cases, concentrates on our customized program methodology of SOA, as we consider SOA a framework for methodology — something a business firm must do, not a product or a technology — something to buy from a technology firm.

The aim of this book is not to define a new methodology for SOA project management but rather to clarify aspects of service-oriented projects that can complement already chosen project management methodologies. The assumption, as cited in frequent literature on SOA,[25] is that one can enhance elements of existing methodologies to integrate service orientation. Another assumption and distinction of the book is that the methodology is technology-neutral, but Section 3 does provide listings of service technology firms and software technologies. The other assumption is that the reader is already cognizant of concepts of service orientation and SOA, Web services, and eXtensible Markup Language (XML) technologies, which are explained fully in books currently on the market and referenced in the Notes after the strategy (Section 1), methodology (Section 2), and technology (Section 3) sections of this book. We also provide references of SOA publications and Web site sources in Section 3 and services terminology in Chapter 10.

Results of Studies on SOA

Results from our current cases of SOA confirm that firms in the studies are continuing to deploy SOA. All of the firms have deployed and expanded Web services based on the principles of SOA. Approximately 50 percent have deployed services, integrated process and services architecture, and restructured organizations and staff. Few have deployed and exploited an SOE because they have not developed the maturity to govern and manage an SOE.

Highlighted below are the results from lessons learned in these cases:

- Close collaboration between the IT department and the business departments can contribute to fast deployment of an SOA solution.
- Enterprise governance of services can ensure effective and economical reusability of services.
- Evolution of functionality on incremental projects, in contrast to "big bang" projects, can be a prudent strategy.
- Focusing on service standards at the beginning of an SOA project can help in the foundation of SOA solutions and SOA strategy.
- Focusing on service orientation training of internal technical and business staff from the beginning of a project is critical for deployment of an SOA strategy.

Lessons learned from these SOA cases confirm, as in our previous study of Web services, that business factors are considered more critical than technical factors in the methodology of an SOA strategy.

These results are explained further in Section 2.

Conclusion

Because of the results, we believe this book can benefit and serve as a reference for business managerial and professional program and project staff considering an extended or initial SOA project. Few books on SOA are designed for business staff. Few books clarify generic SOA methodologies by explaining the criticality of SOA practices in an SOA strategy and furnishing lessons learned from the practices, as is done in this book. Practices of SOA in the firms of our study are evaluated in the business language of our readers. This book is designed for business staff but also can be helpful for technical staff.

Although this book can be construed for large-sized firms extending an SOA project, medium- and small-sized firms and governmental and nonprofit organizations considering adoption of an SOA can benefit from the discipline of the program management methodology; and because of the flexibility of the methodology, they can customize it as needed. Medium- and small-sized firms can benefit from the agility, efficiency, and flexibility in processes just as in large-sized firms if they decide that SOA is an appropriate strategy.

College instructors in an intermediate or advanced course in information systems curricula could concurrently adopt this book. Graduate information systems students who have already learned the foundations of SOA and Web services in a basic course but not business-driven methodology could benefit from the book. Courses on program management methodology and practices of services strategies in industry could improve the currency of instructors and the marketability of information systems students knowledgeable in state-of-the-art techniques.

The authors remain confident that this book will help readers in the likelihood of having substantive and successful SOA strategies.

Notes

1. Anderson, D., Howell-Barber, H., Hill, J., Javed, N., Lawler, J., and Li, Z. 2005. A Study of Web Services Projects in the Financial Services Industry. *Information Systems Management*, Winter, p. 66–76.
2. Daniel, D. 2006. SOA Adoption Gains Momentum. *CIO*, April 15, p. 20.
3. Gruman, G. 2006. Pulling Together an SOA Strategy. *Computerworld*, Next-Gen IT, April: 6.

4. Hurwitz, J. 2006. SOA and Unintended Market Consequences. *CIO*, August 31, p. 1.
5. Birman, K. 2006. The Untrustworthy Web Services Revolution. *Computer*, February, p. 98.
6. Wilson, C. 2006. *Transparent IT: Building Blocks for an Agile Enterprise*. Geniant, LLC, Dallas, Texas, p. 26, 49.
7. Bieberstein, N., Bose, S., Fiammante, M., Jones, K., and Shah, R. 2006. *Service-Oriented Architecture Compass: Business Value, Planning, and Enterprise Roadmap*. Pearson Education, Upper Saddle River, NJ, p. 204.
8. Chang, J.F. 2006. *Business Process Management Systems: Strategy and Implementation*. Auerbach Publications: Taylor & Francis Group, Boca Raton, FL, p. 30, 33.
9. Chang, J.F. 2006. *Business Process Management Systems: Strategy and Implementation*. Auerbach Publications: Taylor & Francis Group, Boca Raton, FL, p. 21.
10. Aberdeen Group, Inc., Boston, MA. 2006. Value of SOA, *Computerworld*, August 7, p. 7.
11. Information Week Research SOA / Web Services Survey. 2006. *Information Week*, September, p. 5.
12. Bieberstein, N., Bose, S., Fiammante, M., Jones, K., and Shah, R. 2006. *Service-Oriented Architecture Compass: Business Value, Planning, and Enterprise Roadmap*. Pearson Education, Upper Saddle River, NJ, p. 215.
13. Bieberstein, N., Bose, S., Fiammante, M., Jones, K., and Shah, R. 2006. *Service-Oriented Architecture Compass: Business Value, Planning, and Enterprise Roadmap*. Pearson Education, Upper Saddle River, NJ, p. 217.
14. Erl, T. 2005. *Service-Oriented Architecture: Concepts, Technology, and Design*. Pearson Education, Upper Saddle River, NJ, p. 37.
15. Krafzig, D., Banke, K., and Slama, D. 2005. *Enterprise SOA: Service-Oriented Architecture Best Practices*. Pearson Education, Upper Saddle River, NJ, p. 69–84.
16. Porter, M.E. 1998. *Competitive Strategy: Techniques for Analyzing Industries and Competitors*. Free Press, New York.
17. Porter. 2001. Strategy and the Internet. *Harvard Business Review*, March, p. 77.
18. Erl. *Service-Oriented Architecture: Concepts, Technology, and Design*, p. 52–54.
19. Chang, J.F. 2006. *Business Process Management Systems: Strategy and Implementation*. Auerbach Publications: Taylor & Francis Group, Boca Raton, FL, p. 49.
20. Bloomberg, J. and Schmelzer, R. 2006. *Service Orient or Be Doomed!: How Service Orientation Will Change Your Business*. John Wiley & Sons, Hoboken, NJ, p. 165.
21. Weill, P. and Ross, J.W. 2004. *IT Governance: How Top Performers Manage IT Decision Rights for Superior Results*. Harvard Business School Press, Boston, MA, p. 54–55.
22. Ross, J.W., Weill, P., and Robertson, D.C. 2006. *Enterprise Architecture as Strategy: Creating a Foundation for Business Execution*. Harvard Business School Press, Boston, MA, p. 9–10, 118–121.
23. Havenstein, H. 2006. SOA Hurdles Forcing Changes in IT Units. *Computerworld*, April 24, p. 1, 12, 14.
24. Beck, K. and Andres, C. 2005. *Extreme Programming Explained, 2nd ed*. Addison-Wesley, Upper Saddle River, NJ.
25. Krafzig, D., Banke, K., and Slama, D. 2005. *Enterprise SOA: Service-Oriented Architecture Best Practices*. Pearson Education, Upper Saddle River, NJ, p. 280.

SERVICE-ORIENTED ARCHITECTURE (SOA) METHODOLOGY

2

Without a program management methodology on a service-oriented project, service-oriented architecture (SOA) would be the wild, wild West.

—Anonymous

Chapter 2

Introduction to Program Management Methodology

To consider the challenge of achieving service-oriented architecture (SOA) in a business firm, this section on SOA methodology begins with an analogy of fiction from the aviation industry.

Assume you are a pilot (i.e., chief executive officer [CEO] of a firm) attempting to fly an airplane (current process) with different engines (business departments and dedicated information technology [IT] departments). The engines are different ages and dimensions (technologies) built by different manufacturers (platform technology firms [vendors]). The engines have been added to the airplane, as the airplane has to fly further distances to more cities (business functions). The engines have been attached above and below the wings of the airplane (applications), in the order that they were built by the manufacturers, with attempts to balance the load on the structure of the wings, as the wings have been customized to the airplane (data center operations). Each of the engines has a distinct repair crew (development staff of the technology departments). A few of the crews (maintenance staff of the technology departments)

27

have been educated on each of the engines, and almost all the crews (development staff) have had experience on the engines with experts in the industry (consultant staff of technology firms). Almost all the engines have distinct fuel (executive sponsors), but a few share fuel with other engines on the airplane. All the engines have distinct nozzles (infrastructure services of the technology departments) to refuel the airplane.

The engines are controlled by different co-pilots (technology teams), and a few of the co-pilots control more than one engine. Each of the co-pilots communicates in a different language, generally the language (current compliance, engineering, finance, human resources, logistics, manufacturing, marketing, sales service, and supply functions) of the country of the manufacturer. Each of the co-pilots has limited control of the navigation of the airplane, in proportion to the power of the engine that he controls, and he may give up the navigation to the pilot. Flight coordination funnels the power into one power stream (organization of firm). This is a challenge because not all the engines may function on a flight (application failures). To address the challenge, a special engine (web services) has been added to one of the wings to improve the power stream, but the engine is balanced on the far end of the one wing. Because of this unanticipated burden, the pilot can fly around in circles in flight (technical solution without a business solution). None of the co-pilots are eager to give up their positions (politics) on the airplane to attempt correcting the location of the added engine, because they must co-pilot the airplane.

Attempting to fly the airplane otherwise (current process) continues to be a concern of the pilot (CEO). The communications of the airplane has flight instructions (terminology) in the different languages of the co-pilots (technology teams). Each of the co-pilots has to activate a recording of "power up" to start the engines. When the pilots power up the engines, they "transfer control" in their languages to the pilot, so that the pilot can fly the airplane. The pilot must fly low (current process), due to fuel inefficiency from the numerous engines, and slow (current process), due to the extra load of the engines. Because the pilot is flying low, she has to navigate geographic features near the ground (infrastructures and organizations) and is impacted by frequent bird migrations (competitors), limited visibility (industry trends), and poor weather (regulations). Because the pilot is flying slower, she does not arrive at her destinations on schedule (business strategy). If the pilot attempts to increase the speed of the airplane to arrive on schedule (reorganization), she has to have agreement of the co-pilots (technology teams). If a co-pilot does not agree with the pilot, he can decrease his portion of the navigation or the power stream (politics), further delaying the flight. If by chance the passengers (customers) on the airplane ask about the arrival schedule, or demand movies, meals, and free drinks in the interim, attendants (customer care representatives) can answer only with: "You are not in an SOE! You are not on SOA Airlines!"

The complexity described in this analogy is akin in various aspects to conditions that might exist in firms contemplating SOA in a not-ready, service-oriented enterprise (SOE).

Background

The background of our methodology is based on the challenge of dealing with the complexity of delivering a *fully deployed* SOA in an SOE, as depicted in the above analogy of aviation. To do SOA in an SOE, a business firm must consider deployment of SOA — not from a single project, but from a number of continued projects evolving in iterations and incremental department, business unit, internal firm and external firm solutions with SOA.[1]

Projects of SOA in this book will evolve from the following levels:

- Department and business unit expansion of Web services to deployment of services, based on a low maturity of SOA; to
- Integration of process and services architecture and restructuring of organizations and staff; and to
- Deployment and exploitation of enterprise services, based on a high maturity of SOE.

To do a non-SOA project, the technology departments of firms have an established *project management methodology* for a project for a fixed outcome on the project. To do SOA, one can define a *program management methodology* for a program for evolving outcomes and projects of SOA that are progressing toward an SOE.

Definition of Program Management Methodology for SOA

Our program management methodology is defined as *Methodology for Enabling Service-Oriented Architecture* (MESOA), a method for an evolutionary SOE. The methodology is described in frameworks of best practices for participant technical, business, and corporate staff on projects of SOA. The frameworks of this methodology, displayed in Figure 2.1, consist of governance, communications, product realization, project management, architecture, data management, service management, human resource management, and post implementation, which are coupled or related tasks for managing a program or a project of SOA.

Although the analysis and design, development, integration and testing, and deployment and implementation phases in the framework of product realization may be equivalent in a project management or project planning methodology, the framework is coupled in service orientation with the other frameworks in our methodology, distinguishing it from project management methodology.

These frameworks furnish principles of service orientation and SOA that can be customized in the project management methodologies with this program management methodology.

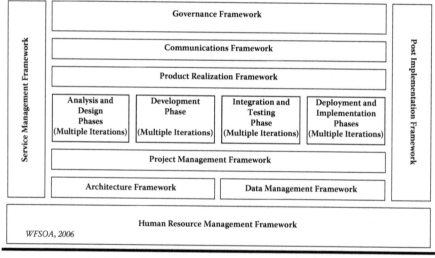

Figure 2.1 Methodology for Enabling Service-Oriented Architecture (MESOA).

The frameworks of our methodology evolve as the programs evolve in iterative phasing and in incremental steps toward an SOE. The frameworks are flexible for changing process requirements and technologies and for further releases of services. For a firm beyond exploration and deployment of pilot projects of Web services, the formalization of the frameworks of our methodology enables the evolution of SOA in a fulfillment strategy toward SOE. Interaction of business staff and technical staff is critical in a fulfillment strategy. The frameworks for the strategy are defined, discussed, and displayed next in Figures 2.2 through 2.10.

Frameworks of Program Management Methodology for SOA

Figures 2.2 through 2.10 depict the sequence of the frameworks of our methodology as sequential, but deployment of the frameworks on projects may be necessarily nonsequential. Firms not having governance or communications as formal frameworks in a *low maturity of SOA* might initiate projects in the product realization framework, based on prioritization of service management requirements and SOA strategy in the service management framework, and realize their initial projects with the architecture and data management frameworks as they refine the requirements. From these initial projects, as the firms learn best practices of SOA and pilot SOA, later projects might evolve in governance and communications as formal frameworks in a *high maturity of SOA*; include the product realization, project management, architecture, data management, and service management frameworks; and integrate the human resource management and post implementation frameworks, as the sequence of the methodology.

Framework of Governance

The framework of governance (Figure 2.2), as described in Chapter 1, enables the alignment of processes and services with business strategy and results in evolution to a service-oriented enterprise (SOE). Governance on projects of SOA ensures that technical and business services conform to a consistent corporate SOA strategy that supports the business strategy of the firm. Because of the evolution in the maturity of projects of SOA, business and technical staff on a project must learn new project management methods, if not unlearn old methods,[2] and governance facilitates learning of program management methodology. Governance ensures faster project

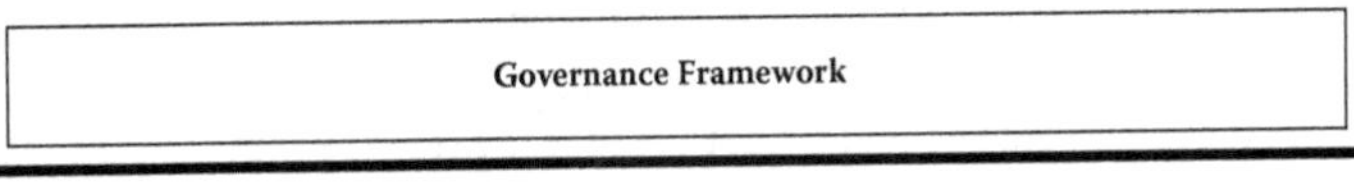

Governance Framework

Figure 2.2 Framework of governance.

implementation of future services, due to new customer, market, or regulatory requirements.[3] The framework of governance enables the goals of SOA.

Governance in our methodology is enabled in a centralized created group of business and technical staff. This group controls a service catalog, containing a registry of current services and a registry of the descriptions of the services, which help in the governance of services. Although the group is critical in the control of services, it may or may not be formalized as a governance group of SOA in early project stages. Formalization of the group is recommended as a strategy. This group in our methodology reports to senior management of the firm.

Framework of Communications

The framework of communications (Figure 2.3) enables emphasis on the *business criticality* of SOA in the firm, which is articulated by the chief information officer (CIO), if not the chief executive officer (CEO), of the firm. Communications on a project of SOA ensures collaboration of business and technical staff in a continued plan on the endeavor in the firm, coupled with the frameworks of our program management methodology. Common reference of technical and business terminology in the firm is critical on projects of SOA.

Communications in our methodology may be enabled in a dashboard designed as a balanced scorecard[4] and displayed on a Web-based portal devoted to SOA or on a business-to-employee (B2E) intranet portal. The dashboard may help in informing project staff and senior management staff on project status, if not the progress of SOA. Investing in a knowledge management system may further help in disseminating information.[5] From such a system, practices of past projects of Web services or SOA can be accessed by project staff and applied to current projects.[6] This framework of communications enables knowledge sharing.

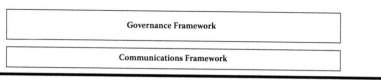

Figure 2.3 Framework of communications.

Framework of Product Realization

The framework of product realization (Figure 2.4) enables the analysis and design, development, integration and testing, and deployment and implementation of SOA and is the core of established project management methodology. Product realization on a project of SOA is coupled with the other established frameworks of our methodology and ensures the focus of the projects is on *business processes* that

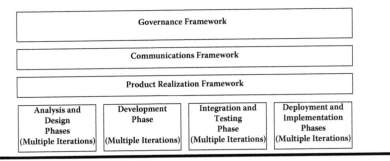

Figure 2.4 Framework of product realization.

will evolve into SOA and not on technology. The program to be realized can be implemented in interlinked iterations of internal department application projects to external firm process integration projects, but the iterations may or may not be sequential. Projects are prioritized and sequenced in the strategy. The framework ensures application of consistent Web services best practices on the projects. This framework that realizes the potential of SOA is controlled by the business unit and department staff with the dedicated help of the technical staff.

Product realization complements chosen agile or complex agile project management methodology already existent in the technology department. In the framework is a mix of complex agile methods or simple agile methods that integrate service orientation in an approach customized to the firm. The framework enables lessons learned from the mix on current project implementations to be applied to future iterative projects of SOA.

Framework of Project Management

Project management as a framework (Figure 2.5) enables delivery of projects of SOA. This framework ensures that changes in business strategy are applied as appropriate on a project of SOA. Project management further ensures that processes and services are functioning and implemented as planned in the strategy. This framework facilitates interaction of technical staff with business staff and helps project teams. Integration of evolving technologies on projects is a function of the framework.

A new age project manager experienced, if feasible, in SOA enables project management. Due to the frequent failure of initiatives in business transformation[7] of firms, a project manager knowledgeable in process transformation and program management methodology, not only project management methodology, is critical on an SOA project. Project management is helped by the knowledge management[8] and dashboard metric portal systems in the above communications framework, which monitor process, project, and service statistics.

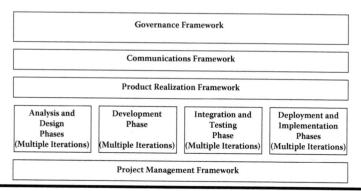

Figure 2.5   Framework of project management.

Framework of Architecture

Architecture as a framework (Figure 2.6) enables compliance of business processes with an SOA model. Architecture on an SOA project ensures evolution from conversion of functions into services, creation of component services and integration into composite services, integration of internal applications, internal services and external services, to on-demand services in a gradual SOE. This framework ensures *seamless integration* of hardware and software that conform to service standards and technology. The framework facilitates improvement of the scalability, performance, and capacity of the infrastructure of SOA from technologies, tools, and utilities of the platform technology firms. Architecture is enabled foremost by an infrastructure architect and security specialist in the evolution of the projects of services to SOA.

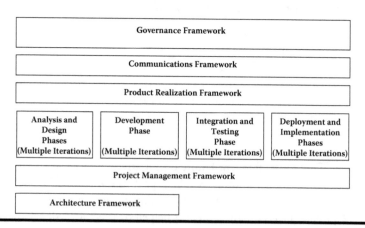

Figure 2.6   Framework of architecture.

Framework of Data Management

The framework of data management (Figure 2.7) enables behaved SOA data services that do not disrupt applications of the firm. Data management on a project of SOA enables implementation of the services, based on access, availability, breadth, and accuracy of data already in the databases of the applications. This framework ensures consistency of data and control of data redundancy and fractal data replication.[9] The database analyst controls the data dictionaries and the metadata catalogs, containing descriptions of information in the databases of the firm, and XML schema catalogs. The framework ensures that the capacity, performance, and scalability of the databases facilitate the requirements of services in an SOA. Data management is enabled by the database administrator and database developers, in addition to the database analyst, all of whom are frequently knowledgeable of the business processes of the firm.

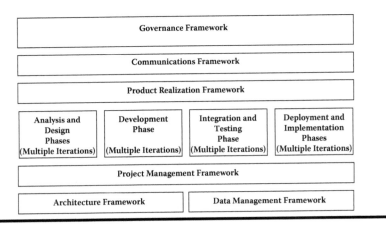

Figure 2.7   Framework of data management.

Framework of Service Management

The framework of service management (Figure 2.8) enables continued conformity and coordination of processes and services to the business strategy defined in the above framework of governance. This framework couples with the aforementioned framework of product realization on a new project of SOA. This ensures that requirements for new processes and new services or revisions to them are not redundant with existing processes or services. The framework ensures reusability of services. Feasibility of processes and services, and impact on the firm, are evaluated in service management. Service management further monitors the performance, scalability, and security of the services and technologies, based on service level agreements (SLAs) between the consumers of the services and the providers of the

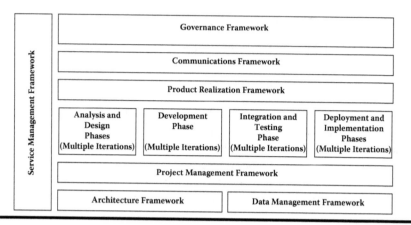

Figure 2.8 Framework of service management.

services. Service management is enabled foremost by business analysts, coordinators of process, and enterprise architects.

Framework of Human Resource Management

The framework of human resource management (Figure 2.9) enables identification of new and revised responsibilities and roles of business and technical staff on SOA. This framework on a project of SOA couples with the other frameworks in our methodology. This ensures that education of the business and technical staff on the business and change in culture of service orientation, and the technical staff on the

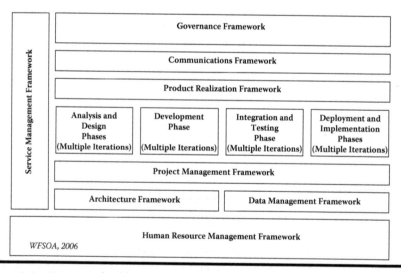

Figure 2.9 Framework of human resource management.

technology of SOA, is furnished throughout the projects of SOA. Human resource management emphasizes organization transformation[10] but integrates technology transformation. This framework facilitates learning of service orientation and of SOA and is enabled by personnel specialists and training specialists.

Framework of Post Implementation

Post implementation as a framework (Figure 2.10) enables service and process life-cycle tasks following product realization. The framework ensures availability of the applications and services and of the technologies, tools, and utilities of SOA. These are formulated in service level agreements (SLAs) between the technology depart-ment, the internal business departments and business units, and the external firms. The agreements are exact in indicating availability (e.g., 99.9 percent 9:00 a.m. to 9:00 p.m.), recovery in the event of downtime (e.g., 30 minutes), response (e.g., 1 second 99.9 percent of the time), and restoration (e.g., 1 hour). This framework enables the organization of the firm to have full advantage of SOA.

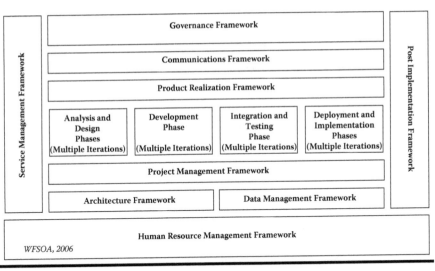

Figure 2.10   Framework of post implementation.

Framework Summary

These frameworks of governance, communications, product realization, proj-ect management, architecture, data management, service management, human resource management, and post implementation furnish the principles of service orientation and SOA in our methodology for an evolutionary SOE. To concretize the frameworks on projects of SOA, business, procedural, and technical factors that enable an SOA strategy are furnished in the frameworks. The factors of the frameworks are defined next.

Business, Procedural, and Technical Factors for Enabling Frameworks of Methodology

The factors for enabling the frameworks of governance, communications, product realization, project management, architecture, data management, service management, human resource management, and post implementation, and for evolving from deployment and expansion of Web services based on SOA to deployment and exploitation of enterprise services based on SOE, are business, procedural, and technical, as cross-referenced and displayed in Table 2.1. These factors are defined in Table 2.2.

These technical, procedural, and business factors are *critical success factors* for fulfilling an SOA strategy with corporate, business, governance, and technical sector staff. The responsibilities and roles of the staff are defined next.

Responsibilities and Roles of Program Staff for Fulfilling Methodology

The responsibilities for fulfilling the factors and frameworks of our methodology are corporate, business, governance, and technical sector staff, as cross-referenced and displayed for a large-sized firm in *full scope* in Table 2.3. The roles of the staff are defined in Table 2.4.

The corporate, business, governance, and technical sector staff are critical staffing for fulfilling an SOA strategy. This staffing may be further formed into a number of formal or informal teams. An example might be application developers, legacy adaptation developers, integration specialists, software architects, and technical documentalists with a technology team leader on a product realization team. To evolve the firm from a low maturity of department and business unit Web services based on SOA to a high maturity of enterprise services based on SOE, the firm may inevitably restructure information technology and business unit organizations. The restructuring of organizations might be similar to the sector staffing and teaming in our methodology.

Framework, Factor, and Staffing Summary

The governance, communications, product realization, project management, architecture, data management, service management, human resource management, and post implementation frameworks; the business, procedural, and technical factors;

and the corporate, business, governance, and technical sector staffing form the foundation of our program management methodology, from which we conducted our analysis of case studies, and our approach to the studies is discussed next.

Approach to Case Studies of Methodology of SOA

From January 2005 to March 2007, we conducted an analysis of 15 Fortune 10 to Fortune 1000 firms, based on available information on each of the firms in generic industry literature and on specific interaction with program staff in a limited number of the firms.

Firms were chosen from evidence of deployment of Web services based on SOA (five firms); deployment of services, integration of process and services architecture, and restructuring of organizations and staff (eight firms); and deployment of services based on SOE (two firms). Deployments in the firms were examples of commonly encountered practices in industry that were evaluated by us with our program management methodology. Firms covered the automobile (one firm), banking (three firms), energy (one firm), health (one firm), insurance (two firms), manufacturing (one firm), technology (two firms), telecommunications (two firms), training (one firm), and travel and leisure (one firm) industries. These firms were headquartered in the United States.

Although the bulk of the firms in the studies were large-sized businesses ($30 billion high [in sales]), a norm in SOA, a few were medium-sized to small-sized firms ($300 million low).

We analyzed the deployment projects on services in each of the firms, beginning with each of the governance, communications, product realization, project management, architecture, data management, service management, human resource management, and post implementation frameworks of our methodology.

To the frameworks were applied an evaluation by us of each of the *projects* perceived by us to be effectively enabled at a high, intermediate, or low level of the methodology or not enabled at all. The evaluation highlighted for illustration key business, procedural, and technical factors on the projects that we perceived as having contributed most effectively to SOA strategy. Each project in the firms was evaluated individually as to its specific factor applicability to our methodology without reference to the circumstantial specificity of the other projects of the firms, so that factors important on each project were identified only in the specificity of each project. This evaluation also identified for illustration program responsibilities and roles of key technical, business, and corporate staff and key technologies that we perceived as having mostly enabled the projects or strategy. The analyses concluded with key lessons learned and levels of maturity of SOA on each of the projects in the studies.

Our analysis and approach were reviewed independently and individually by technology-agnostic colleagues at Pace University and in industry who averaged

30+ years in applied practices of business process management (BPM), program management and project management procedures, and service technologies. The approach was developed from our analysis of Web services projects in 2003 and 2004, from which project studies were published in *Information Systems Management* in winter 2005. This approach was enhanced from a preliminary application of our methodology by us on a sample of firms in 2005, which was presented at the Computational Finance Conference of the Wessex Institute of Technology in London in 2006 and reviewed at a special session of the conference by colleagues from several universities.

We continue to conduct case studies of Web services and SOA with industry-employed graduate students in our *issues in information systems course*, at the Ivan G. Seidenberg School of Computer Science and Information Systems at Pace University, in New York City. We hold focus groups with colleagues and students on Web services and SOA. We systematically review the literature of the business, consulting, and technical press, proceedings of business and technical conferences, and publications of scholarly sources on SOA and Web services.

We now share the relevance of our program management methodology in the results of our 2005–2007 studies in Chapter 3, "Deployment and Expansion of Web Services Based on SOA"; Chapter 4, "Deployment of Services, Integration of Process and Services Architecture, and Restructuring of Organizations and Staff"; and Chapter 5, "Deployment and Exploitation of Services Based on SOE." Results are summarized in Chapter 6, "Conclusion," which ends this section on SOA Methodology.

Table 2.1 Factors for Enabling Frameworks of Methodology

Factors	Frameworks of Methodology								
	Governance	Communications	Product Realization	Project Management	Architecture	Data Management	Service Management	Human Resource Management	Post Implementation
Business Factors									
Agility, efficiency, and flexibility benefits	■	■	■	■	■		■		
Financial benefits	■	■	■	■	■		■		■
Business client participation	■	■	■	■	■	■	■		■
Competitive, market, and regulatory differentials	■	■	■	■	■	■	■		■
Customer demand	■	■	■	■			■		■
Culture of innovation	■	■	■	■	■		■	■	■
Organizational change management	■	■	■	■	■	■	■	■	■
Executive sponsorship	■	■					■	■	
Executive business leadership	■	■	■	■			■	■	■
Executive technology leadership	■	■	■	■	■	■	■	■	■
Strategic planning	■	■	■	■	■	■	■	■	■
Enterprise architecture	■	■	■	■	■	■	■	■	■
Focus on improvement of process	■	■	■	■	■	■	■	■	■
Service orientation	■	■	■	■	■	■	■	■	■
Reusability of assets	■	■	■	■	■	■	■		

Table 2.1 (continued) Factors for Enabling Frameworks of Methodology

Factors	Governance	Communications	Product Realization	Project Management	Architecture	Data Management	Service Management	Human Resource Management	Post Implementation
Procedural Factors									
Control of program	■	■	■	■	■	■	■	■	■
SOA center of competency	■	■	■	■	■	■	■	■	■
Responsibilities and roles	■	■	■	■	■	■	■	■	■
Education and training	■	■	■	■	■	■	■	■	■
Knowledge exchange	■	■	■	■	■	■	■	■	■
Change management	■	■	■	■	■	■	■	■	■
Information management	■	■	■	■	■	■	■	■	■
Common reference	■	■	■	■	■	■	■		■
Naming conventions	■	■	■	■	■	■	■		■
Procurement of technology	■		■	■	■	■	■	■	■
Technology firm knowledge capture	■	■	■	■	■	■	■	■	■
Risk management	■		■	■	■	■	■		■
Standards management	■	■	■	■	■	■	■		■
Infrastructure architecture	■	■	■	■	■	■	■		■
Process and service deployment environment	■	■	■	■	■	■	■		
Process and service deployment techniques	■	■	■	■	■	■	■	■	■

Table 2.1 (continued) Factors for Enabling Frameworks of Methodology

Factors	Frameworks of Methodology								
	Governance	*Communications*	*Product Realization*	*Project Management*	*Architecture*	*Data Management*	*Service Management*	*Human Resource Management*	*Post Implementation*
Service catalog management	■	■	■	■	■	■	■	■	■
Service management and support	■	■	■	■	■	■	■		■
Security management	■	■	■	■	■	■	■	■	■
Continuous process improvement	■	■	■	■	■	■	■	■	■
Costing techniques	■	■	■	■	■	■	■	■	■
Strategy management	■	■	■	■	■	■	■	■	■
Technical Factors									
Internal Web services on project	■	■	■	■	■	■	■		■
Internal process domain on project	■	■	■	■	■	■	■		■
Internal SOA domain on project	■	■	■	■	■	■	■		■
External process domain on project	■	■	■	■	■	■	■		■
External SOA domain on project	■	■	■	■	■	■	■		■
Business process management software	■	■	■	■	■		■	■	■
Data tools	■	■	■	■	■	■	■	■	

Table 2.1 (continued)   Factors for Enabling Frameworks of Methodology

Factors	Frameworks of Methodology								
	Governance	Communications	Product Realization	Project Management	Architecture	Data Management	Service Management	Human Resource Management	Post Implementation
Middleware	■	■	■	■	■	■	■		■
Platform of key technology firms	■	■	■	■	■	■	■		■
Platform specialty tools from platform technology firm	■	■	■	■	■	■	■	■	■
Proprietary technologies	■	■	■	■	■	■	■	■	■
Best-of-class tools	■	■	■	■	■	■	■	■	■
XML standard	■	■	■	■	■	■	■	■	■
Messaging standards	■	■	■	■	■		■		■
Service description and discovery standards	■	■	■	■	■		■		■
Transaction standards	■	■	■	■	■	■	■		■
Security standards	■	■	■	■	■	■	■	■	■
User interface standards	■	■	■	■	■		■		■
Web services best practices	■	■	■	■	■	■	■	■	■
Web services management standards	■	■	■	■	■		■		■

Note: Factors may be cross-referenced to more than one framework in our methodology.

Table 2.2   Definition of Factors for Enabling Methodology

Factors	Description of Factors
Business Factors	
Agility, efficiency, and flexibility benefits	Extent to which benefits of adjusting to business environments drive the program
Financial benefits	Extent to which benefits of increased revenues or decreased expenses drive the program
Business client participation	Extent to which business departments consent, contribute, and furnish content and guidance to the program
Competitive, market, and regulatory differentials	Extent to which competitive, market, and regulatory first-mover edge for the firm drives the program
Customer demand	Extent to which customer demand for enhanced service from technology drives the program
Culture of innovation	Extent to which innovation in business and technical practices is encouraged and facilitates the program
Organizational change management	Extent to which cultural change management is evident in helping business and technical staff embrace the program
Executive sponsorship	Extent to which senior managers in the firm articulate and evangelize the business criticality of SOA as a strategy and fund the program
Executive business leadership	Extent to which senior managers in the business units evangelize business criticality of SOA as a strategy
Executive technology leadership	Extent to which senior managers in the technology departments evangelize the technical and business criticality of SOA as a strategy
Strategic planning	Extent to which business strategy of SOA is articulated in the firm and is accepted by program staff
Enterprise architecture	Extent to which formal enterprise architecture contributes to initiation of the program and evolves with processes to an SOA

Table 2.2 (continued)   Definition of Factors for Enabling Methodology

Factors	Description of Factors
Focus on improvement of process	Extent to which improvement of business processes, process integration, and service choreography are the goals of the program
Service orientation	Extent to which technical and business staff is receptive to principles of service orientation and SOA
Reusability of assets	Extent to which multiple services using software technologies is a goal of the program
Procedural Factors	
Control of program	Extent to which a formal function is evident for guiding and helping the firm in evolution to SOA
SOA center of competency	Extent to which a centralized team is evident for furnishing SOA expertise help to program staff
Responsibilities and roles	Extent to which responsibilities and roles of staff on the program are clearly defined for completing project tasks
Education and training	Extent to which formal skill training on services and SOA is evident for program staff
Knowledge exchange	Extent to which processes and procedures are evident for informing business and technical staff of progress of the program
Change management	Extent to which procedures are evident for ensuring optimal resolution of requests for changes in existing processes or services or of requests for new processes or services
Information management	Extent to which procedures are evident for ensuring data integrity and quality for technical and business functions
Common reference	Extent to which business and technical terminology is applied consistently by program staff
Naming conventions	Extent to which naming standards and service versioning are used by program staff

Table 2.2 (continued)   Definition of Factors for Enabling Methodology

Factors	Description of Factors
Procurement of technology	Extent to which a formal function is evident for furnishing quality hardware and software technology to the program in a cost-effective and expeditious manner
Technology firm knowledge capture	Extent to which program staff captures knowledge from hardware and software technology firms to become independent of the firms
Risk management	Extent to which procedures are evident for mitigating failure or loss caused by SOA
Standards management	Extent to which program staff is cognizant of official standards, scope of implementation of the standards by technology firms and standard gap resolution techniques
Infrastructure architecture	Extent to which procedures are evident for guiding the evolution of technology in a strategy of SOA
Process and service deployment environment	Extent to which procedures are evident for furnishing software and tools to the development staff on the program
Process and service deployment techniques	Extent to which procedures are evident in order to ensure the highest quality of deployed technology throughout the program
Service catalog management	Extent to which procedures for managing a registry or a repository of processes and services are evident on the program
Service management and support	Extent to which procedures are evident for ensuring service availability and reusability and furnishing metrics on service support
Security management	Extent to which procedures are evident for safeguarding access to services
Continuous process improvement	Extent to which procedures are evident for iterative improvement of existing and new processes
Costing techniques	Extent to which techniques are evident for costing existing and future SOA product realization and support

Table 2.2 (continued)   Definition of Factors for Enabling Methodology

Factors	Description of Factors
Strategy management	Extent to which procedures are evident for evaluating and improving program strategy of SOA as required
Technical Factors	
Internal Web services on project	Extent to which Web services as simple projects contribute to the evolution of SOA
Internal process domain on project	Extent to which complex Web services applications contribute to the evolution of SOA
Internal SOA domain on project	Extent to which standards-compliant, internal, and loosely coupled projects contribute to the evolution of SOA
External process domain on project	Extent to which external tightly coupled and security-sensitive and trusted projects contribute to the evolution of SOA
External SOA domain on project	Extent to which external standards-compliant, loosely coupled, and security-sensitive and trusted projects contribute to the evolution of SOA
Business process management software	Extent to which Web Services-Business Process Execution Language (WS-BPEL) software is included in the program
Data tools	Extent to which data tools supporting eXtensible Markup Language (XML) are included in the program
Middleware	Extent to which an enterprise service bus (ESB) or traditional middleware technology is included on the program
Platform of key technology firms	Extent to which the platforms from key technology firms (e.g., BEA, IBM, and Microsoft) are included in the program
Platform specialty tools from platform technology firm	Extent to which specialty tools of the platform technology firms are included in the program
Proprietary technologies	Extent to which proprietary software is included in the program

Table 2.2 (continued) **Definition of Factors for Enabling Methodology**

Factors	Description of Factors
Best-of-class tools	Extent to which specialty tools from pure-play or third-party technology firms are included in the program
XML standard	Extent to which XML is included in the program
Messaging standards	Extent to which technology supporting Simple Object Access Protocol (SOAP), SOAP Message Transmission Optimization Mechanism (MTOM), and SOAP with Attachments (SwA) or similar standards is included in the program
Service description and discovery standards	Extent to which technology supporting Universal Description, Discovery and Integration (UDDI), Web Services Description Language (WSDL), and Web Services-Policy (WS-P) or similar standards is included in the program
Transaction standards	Extent to which technology supporting Web Services-Composite Application Framework (WS-CAF), Web Services-Choreography Description Language (WS-CDL), and Web Services-Transaction (WS-TX) or similar standards is included in the program
Security standards	Extent to which technology supporting XML Encryption, XML Signature, Web Services-Federation (WS-F), Web Services-Security (WS-S), and WS-Security Policy (WS-SP) or similar standards is included in the program
User interface standards	Extent to which user interface tools or Web Services-Remote Portlets (WS-RP) are included in the program
Web services best practices	Extent to which Web Services-Interoperability (WS-I) is included in the program
Web services management standards	Extent to which Service Provisioning Markup Language (SPML) and Web Services-Distributed Management (WS-DM) are included in the program

Table 2.3 Responsibilities of Program Staff for Enabling Methodology

Staff	Governance	Communications	Product Realization	Project Management	Architecture	Data Management	Service Management	Human Resource Management	Post Implementation
Corporate Sector									
Executive sponsor	■								
Business Sector									
Business sponsor	■		■				■		
Business operations sponsor	■		■				■		
Business visionary			■				■		■
Business client			■				■		■
Business manager			■	■					
Business analyst			■				■		
Business analyst for extended organization							■		
Business process specialist			■				■		
Business documentalist	■		■				■		
Business process coordinator							■		
Business testing specialist			■				■		
Business testing coordinator			■				■		
Business support coordinator									■

Table 2.3 (continued)   Responsibilities of Program Staff for Enabling Methodology

Staff	Frameworks of Methodology								
	Governance	Communications	Product Realization	Project Management	Architecture	Data Management	Service Management	Human Resource Management	Post Implementation
Business process project specialist							■		
Governance Sector									
SOA strategist	■						■		
SOA program coordinator	■						■		
Communications coordinator		■							
Knowledge coordinator		■							
Collaboration facilitator	■								
Finance planner	■								
Project planner	■			■					
Enterprise architect			■				■		■
Process specialist	■		■						
Program methodology specialist	■								
Procurement specialist	■								
Business compliance specialist	■								
Technology compliance specialist	■								
Risk specialist	■		■				■		■

Table 2.3 (continued) Responsibilities of Program Staff for Enabling Methodology

Staff	Frameworks of Methodology								
	Governance	Communications	Product Realization	Project Management	Architecture	Data Management	Service Management	Human Resource Management	Post Implementation
Asset librarian			■				■		
Service librarian	■		■				■		■
Technology knowledge specialist	■								
Technology Sector									
Technical sponsor					■	■	■		
Technical visionary			■				■		■
Technical client			■				■		■
Application project manager			■	■					
Infrastructure project manager				■	■				
Team leader			■						
Infrastructure architect			■		■		■		■
Infrastructure tool expert			■		■				
Software architect			■						
Security specialist			■		■				
Legacy adapter developer			■						
SOA developer			■						
Application developer			■						

Table 2.3 (continued) Responsibilities of Program Staff for Enabling Methodology

Staff	Governance	Communications	Product Realization	Project Management	Architecture	Data Management	Service Management	Human Resource Management	Post Implementation
Database administrator			■				■		
Database analyst			■			■			
Database developer			■			■	■		
Technical testing specialist			■				■		
Integration specialist			■						
Deployment specialist			■						
Help desk			■						■
Technical documentalist			■		■	■			
System manager			■		■				■
Service manager									■
Service domain owner				■					■
Infrastructure availability administrator			■				■		■
Service availability administrator									■
Security administrator	■		■	■	■	■	■	■	■
Tool administrator					■				
Corporate Sector — Other									
Personnel specialist	■	■	■	■	■	■	■	■	■
Training specialist	■	■	■	■	■	■	■	■	■

Table 2.4 Roles of Program Staff for Enabling Methodology

	Definitions
Corporate Sector	
Executive sponsor	Advocates SOA as a program and a strategy and funds governance of SOA as a bona fide function in the firm
Business Sector	
Business sponsor	Approves and funds product realization of projects of SOA requested by business units
Business operations sponsor	Approves and funds business process product realization on projects of SOA requested by business department operations
Business visionary	Envisions the full potential of SOA as a business proposition and articulates business requirements in an SOA strategy
Business client	Defines business process and service requirements and is an eventual consumer of business processes and services
Business manager	Manages business project requirements and schedules in liaison with application project manager to ensure SOA product realization
Business analyst	Defines and formalizes business process and service requirements of SOA in the internal business departments and business units of the firm
Business analyst for extended organization	Defines and formalizes business process and service requirements of SOA with external business units or partnered firms
Business process specialist	Applies advanced knowledge of business process management and tools to design, model, test, and implement processes
Business documentalist	Documents current and future business processes and services of SOA
Business process coordinator	Ensures collective focus on improvement of processes on projects of SOA and helps in deployment of services

Table 2.4 (continued)   Roles of Program Staff for Enabling Methodology

	Definitions
Business testing specialist	Develops and executes testing plans and scripts to validate data, interfaces, and business rules
Business testing coordinator	Coordinates testing of SOA between business staff and technical staff
Business support coordinator	Empowers business consumer staff in constructive service usage
Business process project specialist	Ensures process and service projects are initiated in conformance with SOA business strategy
Governance Sector	
SOA strategist	Creates SOA business strategy as an evolutionary strategy and defines a function of governance to manage the SOA program
SOA program coordinator	Coordinates alignment of projects of SOA with enterprise architecture and business strategy
Communications coordinator	Coordinates evangelization of the SOA program and SOA strategy and defines common terminology for program staff
Knowledge coordinator	Coordinates and ensures infusion of knowledge of service orientation to business staff and technical staff on projects of SOA
Collaboration facilitator	Facilitates constructive and close collaboration of business staff and technical staff on projects of SOA
Finance planner	Controls program budget on projects of SOA and costing techniques on service level agreements (SLAs) between technology departments and business units
Project planner	Advises project managers on project planning of SOA and adjustments and maintains an archive of best practices and worst practices
Enterprise architect	Helps project staff on design of infrastructure, design of services, and reusability of services in an evolutionary SOA strategy

Table 2.4 (continued)   Roles of Program Staff for Enabling Methodology

	Definitions
Process specialist	Models business and technical processes on projects of SOA
Program methodology specialist	Adjusts product delivery procedures and processes in order to ensure a balance of control and flexibility
Procurement specialist	Enables procurement of required SOA technologies from technology firms in a cost-effective and expeditious manner
Business compliance specialist	Maintains documentation of government and industry legal and regulatory requirements and audits compliance
Technology compliance specialist	Maintains documentation of industry organizational and technological standards and performs audits
Risk specialist	Furnishes guidelines for risk management on projects of SOA and informs project managers and staff of technical, market, human, and compliance risks
Asset librarian	Furnishes cross-reference of applications, data, programs, processes, and services on SOA and maintains a catalog for the firm
Service librarian	Maintains the SOA service catalog for the firm
Technology knowledge specialist	Helps in knowledge transfer to staff on projects of SOA
Technology Sector	
Technical sponsor	Funds realization of processes and services on projects of SOA
Technical visionary	Envisions the potential of SOA as a business proposition and formalizes technical requirements in an SOA strategy
Technical client	Defines technical service requirements and is a consumer of technical services
Application project manager	Manages application project requirements and schedules to ensure product realization of SOA

Table 2.4 (continued)   Roles of Program Staff for Enabling Methodology

	Definitions
Infrastructure project manager	Manages infrastructure project requirements and schedules to ensure realization of SOA
Team leader	Manages product realization tasks of project technology teams and furnishes project status to project managers
Infrastructure architect	Advises project staff on infrastructure, collaborates with enterprise architect, and maintains infrastructure for the firm
Infrastructure tool expert	Builds complicated components of infrastructure for composite service usage by project technical staff
Software architect	Enables analysis and design and optional prototyping of project requirements of SOA
Security specialist	Helps project staff on security techniques and technologies
Legacy adapter developer	Converts legacy components of services
SOA developer	Creates service metadata, defines interfaces to services, defines messaging (SOAP), assembles services, and executes unit testing
Application developer	Develops user interfaces to services based on business rules and executes unit testing
Database administrator	Converts logical database design into physical databases and maintains databases
Database analyst	Models logical data requirements and maintains data catalogs and schema catalogs
Database developer	Creates data services with SQL or eXtensible Markup Language (XML)
Technical testing specialist	Develops scripts to test interoperability of services and executes testing with business staff
Integration specialist	Merges components of services for testing and deployment

Table 2.4 (continued)   Roles of Program Staff for Enabling Methodology

	Definitions
Deployment specialist	Does rollout of services and ensures education and training of business staff and technical staff on usage of services
Help desk	Helps technical and business staff in problem resolution on usage of services in SOA
Technical documentalist	Documents services of projects of SOA
System manager	Manages hardware and software infrastructure
Service manager	Ensures availability of production services and schedules support tasks
Service domain owner	Inherits deployed processes and services, and ensures continued collaboration of business staff and technical staff
Infrastructure availability administrator	Maintains and monitors capacity, scalability, and performance of SOA infrastructure
Service availability administrator	Maintains and monitors availability of services in consumer business units of the firm through service metrics
Security administrator	Maintains and monitors security of services in SOA
Tool administrator	Maintains and monitors infrastructure usage of specialized tools of SOA
Corporate Sector — Other	
Personnel specialist	Supports SOA by identifying organizational obstacles on projects of SOA and initiating remedial solutions
Training specialist	Maintains organizational support of SOA by implementing required training on service orientation and SOA

Note: Responsibilities and roles may develop from a *partial scope* in deployment of Web services based on SOA, escalate in deployment of services, integration of process and services architecture, and restructuring of organizations and staff, and evolve to *full scope* in deployment of services based on SOE. Such responsibilities may be consolidated in medium- and small-sized firms, so that there might be a lesser number of formal roles in those firms than in large-sized firms.

Notes

1. Havenstein, H. 2006. Small SOA Projects Can Show Immediate ROI. *Computerworld*, October 9, p. 6.
2. Murch, R. 2000. *Project Management: Best Practices for Information Technology (IT) Professionals*. Prentice Hall, Upper Saddle River, NJ, p. 112.
3. Wagner, S. and Dittmar, L. 2006. The Unexpected Benefits of Sarbanes-Oxley. *Harvard Business Review*, April, p. 133–140.
4. Kaplan, R.S. and Norton, D.P. 2005. The Balanced Scorecard: Measures that Drive Performance. *Harvard Business Review*, July, p. 172–180.
5. Murch, R. 2000. *Project Management: Best Practices for Information Technology (IT) Professionals*. Prentice Hall, Upper Saddle River, NJ.
6. Darling, M., Parry, C., and Moore, J. 2005. Learning in the Thick of It. *Harvard Business Review*, August, p. 84–92.
7. Sirkin, H.L., Keenan, P., and Jackson, A. 2005. The Hard Side of Change Management. *Harvard Business Review*, October, p. 108–118.
8. Murch, R. 2000. *Project Management: Best Practices for Information Technology (IT) Professionals*. Prentice Hall, Upper Saddle River, NJ.
9. Fuller, T. and Morgan, S. 2006. Data Replication as an Enterprise SOA Anti-pattern. *The Architecture Journal*, 8, p. 16.
10. Edmondson, A., Bohmer, R., and Pisano, G. 2001. Speeding Up Learning. *Harvard Business Review*, October, p. 125–132.

Chapter 3

Deployment and Expansion of Web Services Based on SOA

This chapter discusses the deployment and expansion of Web services based on SOA in a life insurance firm (Case Study 1), an investment banking firm (Case Study 2), a hardware manufacturing firm (Case Study 3), a hardware and software firm (Case Study 4), and a travel and leisure firm (Case Study 5).

Case Study 1: Life Insurance Firm

Core Project: Internal Department Process

Background of Firm

The firm in Case Study 1 consisted of an established life insurance business. The function of the business was to market basic and customized insurance policies to consumers and distribution channels consisting of 30,000+ agents in the country. The firm focused the marketing of its business on exceptional service to the customers. The concern in the firm in 2004 was that operations could not effectively handle by mail or telephone a higher number of policies or an increased number of regulatory requirements with continued higher service. The process was neither competitively equivalent nor continuously improved for higher expectations of 21st century customer service.

Business Challenge

The process of customer service was non-agile, inefficient, and inflexible in the firm because of legacy methods. Applications were based on an architecture that was brittle, changed for almost each new application, and was not centrally coordinated for different projects by the information technology (IT) department. Applications were developed in batch COBOL language and in nonrelational databases that provided batch extracts to the distribution channels, and development was done with frequently redundant tools. Documentation of the technical applications aligned with the business processes was inconsistent, if not nonexistent. The process of customer service based on exclusively legacy methods and non-Web-based technologies was clearly an impediment to a continuous improvement strategy.

The firm in the study had to deploy an *agile process* so that there would be faster customization and improvement of insurance products, due to customer, partner, and regulatory demands; an *efficient process*, so that there would be empowerment for customers on a Web-based facility; and a *flexible process*, so that there would be improved interaction scaled with an increasing number of customers.

Deployment had to integrate the information in the legacy applications of the firm in an alignment of the architecture with a customer service strategy.

Deployment of Services

The focus of the project was to deploy a flexible, efficient, and agile process for improved customer service. The deployment consisted of architecture of composite applications, component core and current business services, and customer data in an SOA. The services were designed around existent applications that could be accessed by offline and online facilities for self-service by agent partners and customers. These facilities furnished an interface on Web-based portlets installed by Sun Microsystems (eGate and SeeBeyond). The infrastructure for the initial services of the SOA was designed as a reference model for future services.

Higher satisfaction in Web-based service was discerned by the firm in partner and customer surveys in 2006.

Program Management Methodology: Overview

The program management methodology enabled the project with an effective solution of SOA. The methodology frameworks and key factor highlights for Case Study 1 are presented in Figure 3.1 and Table 3.1, respectively.

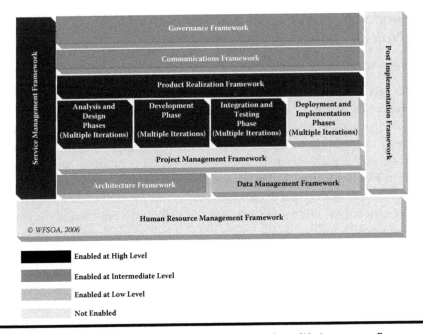

© WFSOA, 2006

■ Enabled at High Level

■ Enabled at Intermediate Level

■ Enabled at Low Level

Not Enabled

Figure 3.1   Methodology frameworks for Case Study 1: life insurance firm.

Table 3.1   Key Factors for Case Study 1

Business Factors	Procedural Factors	Technical Factors
Agility, efficiency, and flexibility benefits	Control of program	Internal SOA domain on project
Competitive, market, and regulatory differentials	SOA center of competency	External SOA domain on project
Customer demand	Responsibilities and roles	Business process management product software
Organizational change management	Knowledge exchange	Data tools
Executive technology leadership	Change management	Middleware
Strategic planning	Common reference	Platform specialty tools from platform technology firm
Focus on improvement of process	Risk management	Proprietary technologies
Service orientation	Infrastructure architecture	Best-of-class tools
Reusability of assets	Process and service deployment environment	XML standard
	Process and service deployment techniques	Messaging standards
		Web services best practices

Note: Definitions of *factors* are given in Table 2.2 in Chapter 2 and may be referenced in more than one framework.

Methodology Frameworks and Key Factor Highlights on Project

Governance

The project was enabled by governance at an intermediate level.

Factors of control of program and strategic planning by the customer service department and by the information technology department were evident in the beginning of the project, and organizational change management, focus on improvement of process, service orientation, reusability of assets, and risk management were evident in the development of responsibilities and roles and in the formation of an SOA center of competency.

Governance was evident as a *bona fide* function for the initiation of the project, but was not fully realized on the project due to a lack of involvement on the part of executive business leadership from the business unit.

Communications

The project was enabled by communications at an intermediate level, in evangelization of services as a process solution by executive technology leadership in the technology department. The department emphasized agility, efficiency, and flexibility benefits; competitive, market, and regulatory differentials; and customer demand of SOA. Knowledge exchange was also an enabling factor. The department focused on the initial integration of customer service strategy with SOA.

Not evident was executive business leadership in promoting a strategy with the communications staff.

Product Realization

The project was enabled by product realization at a generally high level, in process and service deployment environment and process and service deployment techniques, and business process management product software, data tools, platform specialty tools from platform technology firms and proprietary technologies, which facilitated an iterative methodology including prototyping the initial services.

This project included internal SOA domain and external SOA domain.

Project Management

The project was not enabled by formal project management.

Architecture

The project was enabled at an intermediate level by architecture aligned with customer service strategy, in a common reference model for existing and future services, and was further enabled in middleware, XML standard, and messaging standards (Simple Object Access Protocol [SOAP]), but was not fully implemented in an enterprise infrastructure strategy, in order to support the customer service strategy.

Not evident was business client participation on architecture.

Data Management

The project was enabled by data management of the legacy application files of the firm at a low level, as the focus of the project was to adapt the files for agent partners and customers without detailed analysis of the data in the files.

Service Management

The project was enabled by service management at a high level, in the inclusion of infrastructure architecture, based on a customer service model, and was further enabled by change management, best-of-class reengineering tools, and Web services best practices, which helped in integration of legacy applications.

Human Resource Management

The project was not enabled by human resource management. The factor of organizational change management in the framework of human resource management was elusive on the project. Although education and training of the technology department on SOA was furnished by the main technology firm, it focused on the immediate project and the technology, not on the integration of the technology in a business strategy of SOA.

Post Implementation

This project was not enabled by post implementation in the management of services and strategy of SOA, due to the immaturity of the immediate project.

Key Program Roles

Table 3.2 presents the key program roles for Case Study 1.

Table 3.2   Key Program Roles for Case Study 1

Governance Sector SOA strategist Enterprise architect Program methodology specialist Asset librarian Communications coordinator
Technology Sector Technical sponsor Infrastructure architect

Note: Key program roles tables in this section display frequently cited *highest* enabling key roles on the projects from all of the roles of staff in each case study.

Note: Key technologies on the projects are discussed in the technology section of our book.

Summary of Project

The project in Case Study 1 is an example of a process enabled for improvement of customer service, but the process is not fully integrated in a larger SOA strategy.

Key Lessons Learned on Project

- Deployment of services can contribute to immediate process improvement in a tactical SOA solution, but may not ensure an SOA strategy.
- Methods of deployment may be informal in tactical SOA solutions, but may be insufficient in an SOA strategy.

Maturity of SOA on Project

Figure 3.2 illustrates the maturity of SOA for the Case Study 1 project.

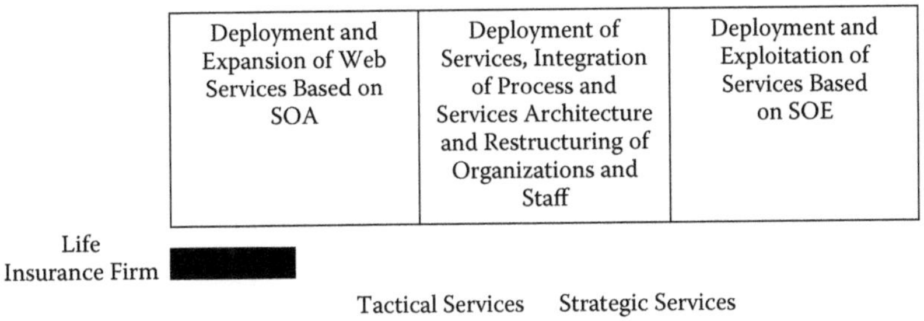

Deployment and Expansion of Web Services Based on SOA	Deployment of Services, Integration of Process and Services Architecture and Restructuring of Organizations and Staff	Deployment and Exploitation of Services Based on SOE
Life Insurance Firm ████████		

Tactical Services   Strategic Services

Figure 3.2   Maturity of SOA for Case Study 1 project.

Case Study 2: Investment Banking Firm
Core Project: Internal Department Process
Background of Firm

The firm in Case Study 2 consisted of an internal department of an investment banking business unit. The function of the department was to execute daily instructions on 100,000+ security trades for customers of investment managers, and to furnish reports on the security markets and the trades to the managers. Investment managers were from large, intermediate, and small-sized financial institutions in domestic and foreign locations.

Although the information and the instructions were delivered in electronic files to the department, the concern of management was that files were fed in diverse entry formats, from industry-defined specific standard messages to Excel spreadsheet and generic Word messages and fax messages. The large-sized institutions fed industry-defined standard formats for automatic entry into the appropriate applications of the department. The intermediate and small-sized institutions frequently fed non-industry defined and non-standard formats, which had to be edited by the department for manual entry into the applications.

Departmental staff had to maintain the internal process of executing the trades and the external reporting on the executed trades from inconsistent files and formats.

Business Challenge

This process was inefficient for the firm, as the execution of the trades from the intermediate and small-sized institutions was delayed due to manual entry by departmental staff. Information, including security codes or ticker symbols, had to be acquired from the institutions sometimes by telephone and entered by the staff. Execution was costly because of having extra staff for this manual step and because of inadvertent errors by the staff in entering the input into the applications.

Errors from information entered manually by the staff were evident in the final reporting of the security trades. Erroneous reporting on the trading delivered to the investment managers in the institutions caused these managers to consider discontinuing business with the firm, although inconsistency in the file formats of their instructions contributed to the erroneous processing and reporting and statistics.

The firm in the study had to deploy *an efficient process* so that there would be fewer errors in the processing and reporting of the trades, and *a flexible process*, so that there would be customized formats from profitable small-sized institutions that preferred such input.

Deployment of Services

The focus of the project was to cut operations costs and to have a flexible and efficient if not agile process of information and instructions from the institutions to the department and of information reporting from the department to the institutions, based on a convenient industry standard. The solution was an SOA for existing institutions delivering instructions of trading to the department. This solution was consistent with Web services standards and was additionally deployable for future institutions that may conduct business with the firm.

The project on SOA furnished an interface on a data exchange Web-based portal to the institutions, in which instructions were fed by the investment managers of the institutions to the diverse applications of the department. This project filtered and integrated the feeds from the institutions into automatic formats that conformed to the Society for Worldwide Inter-Bank Financial Telecommunication (SWIFT) descriptions for entry of such information. Edits in the formats were done in the applications without manual intervention by the departmental staff with cost savings of 60 percent. SOA included a Cape Clear Business Enterprise Service Bus (ESB) Integration Suite for centralized control and management of component format services, online monitoring of the performance of the services, and the reusability of the services.

Fast integration of new institutions was enabled in the SOA in a few hours, not in pre-SOA weeks, without costly coding of the applications behind the services, which furnished a clear improvement in the business of security trading by the firm, in contrast to trading by competitor firms in the financial industry. Information technology staff in the firm was trained on the Cape Clear Suite and on Organization for the Advancement of Structured Information (OASIS) and Web Services – Interoperability (WS-I) standards of technology.

Program Management Methodology: Overview

The program management methodology enabled the project with an effective departmental internal solution of SOA with one vendor. The methodology frameworks and key factor highlights for Case Study 2 are presented in Figure 3.3 and Table 3.3, respectively.

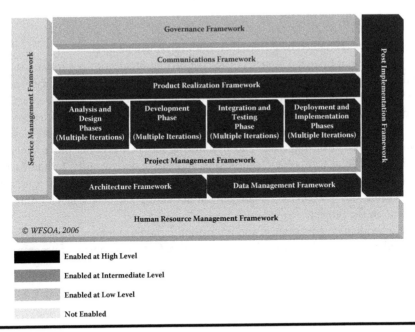

Figure 3.3   Methodology frameworks for Case Study 2: investment banking firm.

Table 3.3   Key Factors for Case Study 2

Business Factors	Procedural Factors	Technical Factors
Agility, efficiency, and flexibility benefits	Information management	Internal process domain on project
Financial benefits	Naming conventions	Internal SOA domain on project
Competitive, market, and regulatory differentials	Procurement of technology	External process domain on project
Customer demand	Risk management	External SOA domain on project
Culture of innovation	Standards management	Business process management product software
Executive technology leadership	Infrastructure architecture	Data tools
Strategic planning	Process and service deployment environment	Middleware
Focus on improvement of process	Process and service deployment techniques	Proprietary technologies
Service orientation	Service management and support	Best-of-class tools
Reusability of assets	Security management	XML standard
	Costing techniques	Messaging standards
		Transaction standards
		Security standards
		Web services best practices
		Web services management standards

Governance

The project was enabled by governance at an intermediate level.

The factor of financial benefits from cost savings on customized instructions of trading was highly evident on the project. Flexibility, efficiency, and agility benefits; competitive, market, and regulatory differentials; and customer demand were also evident on the project. Culture of innovation facilitated investment in SOA and was evident on the project. Service orientation furnished customization, description, exception error, interface, and monitoring services. Product procurement of Cape Clear Suite technology, transaction standards, and security standards in a standards strategy were evident on the project. Executive technology leadership in focusing on Web services management standards and strategic planning was evident on the project.

Not evident on governance, and important in program management methodology and on projects similar to Case Study 2, were factors of control of program and service catalog management.

Communications

The project was not enabled by formal communications, as the focus of the project was a fast deployment of an initial SOA solution; and, because of this focus, technology firm knowledge capture was not evident on the project.

Product Realization

The project was enabled by product realization at a high level.

Business process management software was evident in input formatting logic for the instructions of the institutions. Reusability of assets, standards management, and risk management were evident in an initial services strategy. Process and service deployment environment, process and service deployment techniques, best-of-class tools, and data tools were evident in the integration of the information and the instructions with the applications behind the input process, and Web services best practices were evident in the previously mentioned OASIS WS-I standards.

Project Management

The project was not enabled by the formality of project management planning.

Architecture

The project was enabled by architecture at a high level in internal and external process domains and in internal and external SOA domains of the project of the firm and of the institutions.

Factors included infrastructure architecture, for integrating ESB middleware; and security management, proprietary messaging technologies, messaging standards, and transaction standards, for integrating functions of trading of the intermediate and small-sized institutions.

Data Management

The project was enabled by data management at a high level in factors of information management and naming conventions, which furnished data quality; and XML standard, which facilitated nonredundancy of the data and was highly important in improving the processes.

Service Management

The project largely depended on the external technology firm and was not enabled by full dimensions of service management nor by business client participation, change management, or service management and support as minimum inclusions.

Human Resource Management

The project was not enabled by human resource management, as formalizing responsibilities and roles of the information technology staff and the business staff and furnishing education and training of the technology staff on organizational change management were not included in the project.

Focus on improvement of process in the department was, however, included in the project.

Not included in the project was the factor of change management in furnishing future institutions with services.

Post Implementation

The project was enabled at a high level by a continued and noticeable focus on improvement of process and costing techniques in post implementation, from the beginning of the program management methodology, in the existing institutions.

Key Program Roles

Table 3.4 lists the key program roles for Case Study 2.

Table 3.4   Key Program Roles for Case Study 2

Business Sector	Governance Sector
Business client	Process specialist
Business analyst	
Business support coordinator	**Technology Sector**
Business testing specialist	Technical sponsor
	Security specialist
	Database analyst
	Software architect

Summary of Project

Although governance, product realization, architecture, data management, and post implementation enabled the project in Case Study 2, the project is an example of a departmental SOA; and communications, project management, service management, and human resource management may have to be expanded in the firm to ensure a pathway for a successful SOA strategy.

Key Lessons Learned on Project

- Choice of a *bona fide* SOA technology firm can contribute to fast deployment of a departmental solution, but enterprise expansion of the solution, and additional technology firms, may have to be considered by management.
- Focus on service standards at the beginning of SOA can help in the foundation of SOA solutions and in an SOA strategy.
- Integration of Web services contributes to SOA solutions and SOA strategy.

Maturity of SOA on Project

Figure 3.4 illustrates the maturity of SOA for the Case Study 2 project.

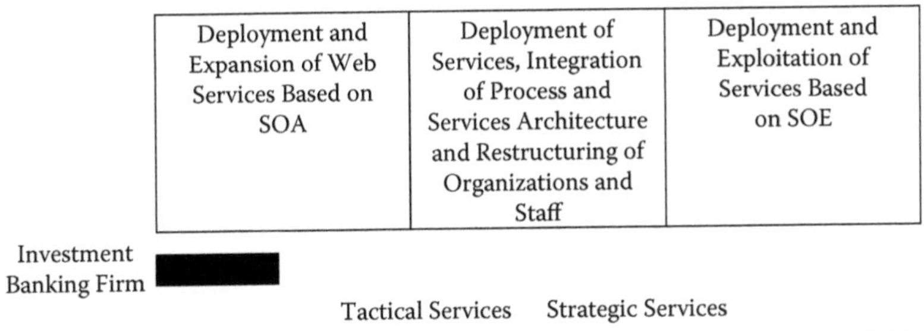

Deployment and Expansion of Web Services Based on SOA	Deployment of Services, Integration of Process and Services Architecture and Restructuring of Organizations and Staff	Deployment and Exploitation of Services Based on SOE

Investment Banking Firm

Tactical Services   Strategic Services

Figure 3.4   Maturity of SOA for Case Study 2 project.

Case Study 3: Hardware Manufacturing Firm

Core Project: Internal Department Process

Background of Firm

The firm in Case Study 3 was a hardware manufacturing business. This firm had an order entry and planning application in 20+ facilities for generating a daily 3000+ orders and 12,000+ materials for domestic and international customers and business partners. The application consisted of batch procedures coded with 2+ million lines of coding, developed in PL/1 in 1978, and enhanced with CICS and Web screen scraping. Input of orders from partners and customers was delayed frequently due to coding or manual processing of customized ordering of new products, which further delayed the delivery of the products. This process was inconsistent for a firm with an external image as leading edge in products.

Business Challenge

The process of fulfilling orders for customers with an essentially noncustomizable application was inefficient and inflexible for the firm. Discrepancies entered into the application caused errors in the batch processing of the orders. Functions for processing new products had to be coded into the application by a dwindling number of PL/1 developers in the information technology department. Inevitably processing was delayed from 1 week to 3 months in delivery of new products to customers and partners. The firm was challenged by these conditions, as competitor firms required between one and five days to deliver products to their partners.

This firm had to deploy an *efficient process,* so that there would be expedited delivery and fewer errors in the processing of orders, and a *flexible process,* so that there would be improved integration in the processing of new products. The firm had to incrementally migrate processing to services. Time-to-market was critical in the deployment of a flexible and efficient process if partners and customers were to continue to do business with the firm.

Deployment of Services

The focus of the project was to have an efficient and flexible ordering process. The solution was an online Web-based portal application extended to the order processing application. The technology department externalized the business logic of the processing and furnished composite services to control and edit errors and inputs of orders. The application continued earlier internal processing; but on the project, problematic routines were redeveloped in Java. The impact of the portal SOA was faster integration of orders and products, faster exception processing of orders, and faster time-to-market of products to customers and partners.

SOA saved 95 percent in time-to-process of orders and 25 percent in the integration of the products into their applications in 2006. Further savings were expected for 2007 to 2009.

Technology included IBM WebSphere Business Integration Server Foundation, Portal, and Studio Developer Integration.

Program Management Methodology: Overview

The program management methodology enabled the firm in this project with an effective solution of SOA. Figure 3.5 presents the methodology frameworks for Case Study 3, and Table 3.5 lists the key factors.

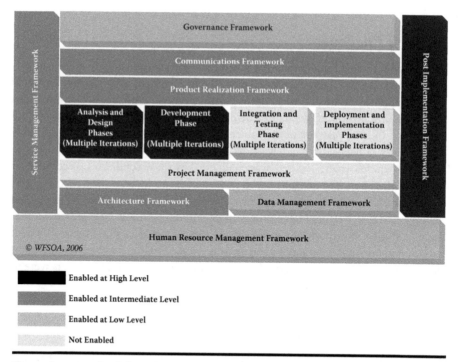

Figure 3.5 Methodology frameworks for Case Study 3: hardware manufacturing firm.

Table 3.5 Key Factors for Case Study 3

Business Factors	Procedural Factors	Technical Factors
Agility, efficiency, and flexibility benefits	Control of program	Internal process domain on project
Financial benefits	Responsibilities and roles	Internal SOA domain on project
Business client participation	Knowledge exchange	External process domain on project
Competitive, market, and regulatory differentials	Change management	External SOA domain on project
	Information management	Business process management product software
Customer demand	Common reference	Data tools
Culture of innovation	Risk management	Middleware
Organizational change management	Infrastructure architecture	Platform of key technology firms
Focus on improvement of process	Process and service deployment environment	Platform specialty tools from platform technology firm
Service orientation	Process and service deployment techniques	Proprietary technologies
Reusability of assets	Service management and support	XML standard
	Security management	Messaging standards
	Continuous process improvement	Service description and discovery standards
	Costing techniques	User interface standards

Governance

The project was enabled by governance at a low level.

Factors of competitive, market, and regulatory differentials in new products in the industry; customer demand; and financial benefits from potential risk reduction of revenue from investment in an SOA were highly evident on this project.

Agility, efficiency, and flexibility benefits and financial benefits were highly evident and helped from the investment on the project. Focus on improvement of process was evident and helped by control of program and risk management. Service orientation in an online portal SOA and reusability of assets in the technology of the offline applications were evident on the project.

Culture of innovation was eventually evident on the project.

Although these factors were evident and frequent in governance, the focus of the project was a portal solution and not strategic planning of an SOA. Thus, governance was of an SOA project and not of an SOA strategy. Service catalog management was also not evident in the project. Control of program was evident but was evolving and was immature in this project.

Communications

The project was enabled by communications at an intermediate level, in factors of common reference and continued knowledge exchange of business staff with the technical staff, which facilitated continuous process improvement in the firm. However, not evident was executive business leadership or executive technology leadership in the promotion of a strategy.

Product Realization

The project was fully enabled by product realization at a generally intermediate level.

Factors of business models with business process management products and data object models with data tools were evident in evaluating the offline and online processing that services would impact. Focus on platform of key technology firms, platform specialty tools from platform technology firms, and proprietary technologies and infrastructure architecture were evident on the project. Process and service deployment environment and process and service deployment techniques were evident on the project. XML standard and service description and discovery standards (UDDI) were evident in iterative project steps.

Internal process domain, internal SOA domain, external process domain, and external SOA domain were included on the project.

Not included and important on product realization were the phases of integration and testing and deployment and implementation.

Project Management

The project was not as effectively enabled by formal project management as by product realization and governance.

Architecture

The project was enabled by architecture at an intermediate level, in infrastructure architecture of the hardware and the software of the initial SOA. Messaging middleware and messaging standards were evident on the project. User interface standards were evident on the portal SOA.

This project was enabled, however, by proprietary technologies, which were not recommended state-of-the-art SOA technologies.

Not evident was strategic planning of the infrastructure, as the project focused on the order processing portal and not on further inclusion of other applications of processes that might be linked into this portal or on integration of nonproprietary technologies.

Data Management

The project was enabled by data management at a low level, in information management of metadata and modeling of the ordering process, but not of other information in other processes that might be improved on projects similar to this.

Service Management

The project was enabled at an intermediate level by business client participation in the prioritization of services and by change management in the criticality of the initial project, but not in expanded service management and support with a dedicated service management staff.

Human Resource Management

The project was enabled at a low level by organizational change management and proper responsibilities and roles of the developer and architect technical staff and of the business consumer and owner staff.

Not evident was a plan for the education and training of the business staff on the business processes implemented on the project.

Post Implementation

The project was enabled at a high level by service management and support, in the monitoring of the performance of the services, to ensure customer and partner satisfaction, and by security management and costing techniques.

Key Program Roles

Table 3.6 presents the key program roles for Case Study 3.

Table 3.6 Key Program Roles for Case Study 3

Business Sector	Technology Sector
Business manager	Infrastructure architect
Business analyst	Software architect
	SOA developer
Governance Sector	Database analyst
Risk specialist	Database developer
Asset librarian	

Summary of Project

Although governance, product realization, and architecture effectively and fully enabled the project in Case Study 3, this project is an example of a limited SOA solution, and service management may have to be enhanced in the firm to evolve services in a full SOA strategy.

Key Lessons Learned on the Project

- Competitive differential and customer demand for efficiency and flexibility in a business can be compelling drivers for a fast SOA solution.
- Externalization of business logic from legacy software can contribute to an effective interim solution and can support an SOA strategy.

Maturity of SOA on Project

Figure 3.6 illustrates the maturity of SOA for Case Study 3 project.

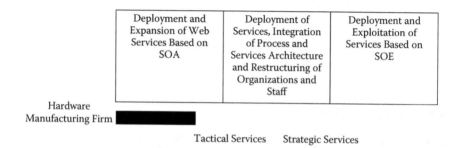

Deployment and Expansion of Web Services Based on SOA	Deployment of Services, Integration of Process and Services Architecture and Restructuring of Organizations and Staff	Deployment and Exploitation of Services Based on SOE

Hardware Manufacturing Firm ▰▰▰▰▰

Tactical Services   Strategic Services

Figure 3.6 Maturity of SOA for Case Study 3 project.

Case Study 4: Hardware and Software Firm

Core Project: Internal Department Process

Background of Firm

The company in Case Study 4 was a hardware and software firm that conducted business with 18+ million consumer customers in 30+ countries. The firm accepted product registrations by mail, telephone, or Web from these customers. Information on purchases was input by customer care representatives of the firm into different identity management applications that interfaced with diverse marketing, sales, and service databases. Information was integrated in a data warehouse and in data marts for data mining of the transactions. The firm collaborated with affiliated firms and product service providers.

Business Challenge

The process of identity management was inefficient for the firm in this study, as information in the data marts was duplicated in the data warehouse. Although there were an actual 18+ million customers, the firm had an inaccurate 26+ million identified in databases, data marts, and data warehouse. Information on customers inherited from firms that merged with this firm was input into databases not integrated with the data marts and data warehouse. The information in the databases, data marts, and data warehouse was maintained in diverse database management systems (DBMSs), which was not efficient for fast mining. Mining of information was not effective in the marketing and servicing of products of technology for high profit potential consumers, as the information was frequently inaccurate due to changes in customer profiles.

This process was further ineffective and inefficient in the management of privacy. Although the firm was distinguished in international privacy policy, isolation of the databases, data marts, and data warehouse hindered management of the policy. Information on 3+ million European and Asian customers was maintained in external databases because of international policies on privacy. The information in the applications was maintained in diverse software, which was inefficient for fast maintenance. Management of privacy was inefficient for international regulations.

The firm in this study had to deploy a competitive and *efficient process* so that there would be improved identity management of information on customers, improved mining of product information on customers, and improved information privacy management.

Deployment of Services

The focus of the project was to improve customer data management and identity management, data mining of information, and international information privacy with a solution of an SOA. The information technology department of the firm deployed algorithmic component data matching services to control duplication of information in the databases, data marts, and data warehouse and to manage identities of the customers in the data marts and the data warehouse. Improved data accuracy was evident from a decrease of $2+ million in maintenance of duplicated databases and data marts and an increase of $25+ million in marketing profit in 2006.

The technology department deployed composite privacy and security services to the applications and federated security and service standards for affiliated firms. Improved privacy and security management in the SOA was evident in applications housing information on international customers and in further distinguishing the firm in privacy standards by the European Union.

The technology department deployed Altova, BEA, IBM, Microsoft, and Oracle in the study.

Program Management Methodology: Overview

The program management methodology enabled the project with an effective and efficient but limited SOA solution. Figure 3.7 illustrates the methodology frameworks for Case Study 4, while Table 3.7 provides the key factors for this case study.

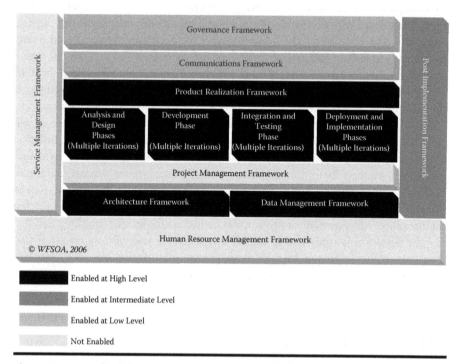

Figure 3.7 Methodology frameworks for Case Study 4: hardware and software firm.

Table 3.7 Key Factors for Case Study 4

Business Factors	Procedural Factors	Technical Factors
Agility, efficiency, and flexibility benefits Financial benefits Competitive, market, and regulatory differentials Culture of innovation Strategic planning Focus on improvement of process Service orientation Reusability of assets	Control of program Responsibilities and roles Information management Common reference Naming conventions Technology firm knowledge capture Risk management Standards management Infrastructure architecture Process and service deployment environment Process and service deployment techniques Service catalog management Service management and support Security management Continuous process improvement Costing techniques Strategy management	Internal process domain on project Internal SOA domain on project External process domain on project External SOA domain on project Business process management product software Middleware Platform of key technology firms Platform specialty tools from platform technology firm Best-of-class tools XML standard Messaging standards Service description and discovery standards Security standards Web services best practices Web services management standards

Governance

The project was enabled by governance at a low level.

Factors of agility, efficiency, and flexibility benefits, competitive, market, and regulatory differentials, and financial benefits were goals in the focus on improvement of process of identity management, mining, and privacy. Costing techniques enabled evaluation of financial benefits from investment in the SOA. Control of program and risk management was facilitated by standards management, service catalog management, security management, and security standards, and strategic planning was helpful on the project.

Not evident and highly important in methodology on projects similar to Case Study 4 were executive business leadership and executive technology leadership in this study.

Communications

The project was enabled by communications in common reference of shared terminology that corrected the inconsistency in data in the databases, data marts, and data warehouse; but apart from this factor as important in communications, knowledge exchange as a procedural factor was not enabling the project.

Communications was essentially at a low level.

Product Realization

The project was enabled by product realization at a high level, in process and service deployment environment, and process and service deployment techniques that focused on the reusability of assets of the applications in the firm. Reusability of European privacy rules was evident and helped in usability of Asian privacy rules. Naming conventions, service catalog management with version control, and Web services best practices helped in publishing data services and in reusing the services.

Project Management

The project was not enabled by formal project management.

Architecture

The project was enabled by architecture at a high level.

Factors of infrastructure architecture and business process management products facilitated service orientation of a process and service deployment environment for current and future services. Web services best practices, including middleware in the form of an ESB, facilitated frequent reconfiguration of services. Specification of service description and discovery standards was instrumental in integrating data into services. Security standards were instrumental in integrating services of the firm with affiliated firms. Best-of-class tools, platform of key technology firms, and platform specialty tools from platform technology firms interoperated with XML standard, messaging standards (SOAP), service description and discovery standards (UDDI), security standards, and Web services management standards.

The firm was enabled from internal process domain and external process domain to internal SOA domain and external SOA domain on the project.

Data Management

The project was enabled exceptionally and highly by data management at a high level.

The information management factor was evident in the beginning of a metadata catalog for all data in the databases, data marts, and data warehouse. The catalog helped in defining correct data for the firm. Importantly, the catalog was deployed as a consolidation service throughout the technology department of the firm and the technology departments of the affiliated firms.

Information entered into the diverse data marts and databases of the applications was edited to the metadata consolidation service, which eliminated 100,000+ redundant inputs monthly in 2006.

Service Management

The project was not enabled by service management.

Not evident on the project was change management — nor a plan.

Human Resource Management

Although the project was enabled in the factors of culture of innovation and limited responsibilities and roles, which facilitated SOA in the firm, and was helped by limited technology firm knowledge capture, it was not enabled in integration of education and training of the technical staff by the technology firms on the project, so that inevitably the project was not enabled by human resource management.

Post Implementation

The project was enabled and helped at an intermediate level by continuous process improvement and service management and support to ensure full integration of data and privacy services, but the enablement focused on metadata services as a solution and not on other services in a continuous process improvement strategy.

Key Program Roles

Table 3.8 defines the key program roles for Case Study 4.

Table 3.8   Key Program Roles for Case Study 4

Governance Sector	Technology Sector
Technology compliance specialist	Database analyst
Service librarian	Security specialist
Program methodology specialist	Database administrator
	Infrastructure architect
	SOA developer

Summary of Project

Although governance, architecture, and data management effectively enabled the project in a controlled deployment of metadata and privacy services, evolution to full SOA may depend on expanded service management — as a philosophy and as a strategy — in Case Study 4.

Key Lessons Learned on Project

- Conscientious data management can contribute to effective deployment of metadata services.
- Control of discrete project services can contribute to a probable SOA solution.
- Deployment of metadata services is an example of an SOA solution but may not be an SOA strategy.

Maturity of SOA on Project

Figure 3.8 illustrates the maturity of SOA for the Case Study 4 project.

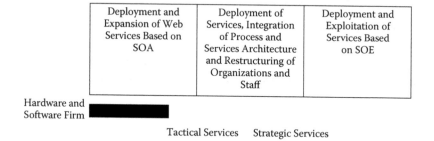

Deployment and Expansion of Web Services Based on SOA	Deployment of Services, Integration of Process and Services Architecture and Restructuring of Organizations and Staff	Deployment and Exploitation of Services Based on SOE

Hardware and Software Firm ████████████

Tactical Services   Strategic Services

Figure 3.8   Maturity of SOA for Case Study 4 project.

Case Study 5: Travel and Leisure Firm

Core Project: Internal Department Process

Background of Firm

The firm in this case study consisted of a large national travel and leisure business of 3000+ agents in 200+ offices, along with a network of 18,000+ independent agents, contributing to a daily 2+ million transactions with travelers in 2006. From 1960 the firm furnished generic travel packages to travelers, but was impacted by the Internet in the 1990s when travelers became enabled to develop customized travel packages on the Web without the help of travel agents. Growth in the number of packages with travelers was even lower in the firm in the 1990s, in contrast to other firms impacted in the industry by the Web.

The firm deployed a process based on Web services that could empower agents to customize packages with travelers quickly, and that could enable travelers to develop their own personal plans instantaneously with applications on the firm's Web site. The goal of the firm was not only to continue business with current travelers, but also to expand the business for future travelers by integrating internal applications with external applications of hotels and airlines already on the Web.

Business Challenge

The process deployed by the firm was ineffective for the business. The managers in the marketing department encouraged agents of the firm to customize packages with travelers in offices or on the telephone, but they discouraged travelers from less profitable personal planning on the firm's Web site. Customized packages developed in the offices were higher in packaged revenue sales.

Although independent agents in the larger network favored personalized planning and customized packaging, they were not considered *bona fide* contributors in decisions of the marketing department not to expand the functionality of personalized planning on the firm's Web site. The promotion of customized packaging by agents in the offices or on the telephone, to the exclusion of personalized planning by travelers on the Web, was inevitably ineffective in expanding the business of the firm with consumer travelers.

This process was also inefficient for the firm. Although the technology department, helped by a consulting firm, deployed Web services behind the customized packaging process, the services were not based on formal requirements defined by the marketing department. The technology department deployed the services based on interpretation of requirements, as requirements were not furnished by the marketing department because of cultural resistance to change in the latter department. The deployment of the services was confined to less than 10 percent of the 3000+ internal agents in the firm, due to a lack of education in the technology department of enterprise architecture and governance of the services. The technology department was not sufficiently trained on the management of the services by the consulting team.

The travel and leisure firm in this study clearly had to deploy a flexible, efficient, and agile process. The firm had to have a *flexible process* so that there would be full functionality for customized packaging by internal and external agents, as well as full functionality for personalized planning by travelers. The firm had to have an *efficient process* so that there would be enterprise governance of shared services for agents and organizations, managed by a technology department knowledgeable in SOA. This firm had to consider having an *agile process* so that there would be agents and managers adaptive to change in business and consumer practices of traveling, due to the impact of Web-based technology.

Having an agile, efficient, and flexible process would enable the firm to continue as a leader in the leisure and travel industry.

Deployment of Services

The focus of this new project was to have a flexible, efficient, and agile process of business. The firm deployed SOA in 2006 as a solution. Services were first furnished to half the 3000+ internal agents, which enabled customized formatting of packaging from information in internal legacy applications. Through composite services, the agents handled single and triangle destination packaging with international and domestic rail, cruise, or airline segments of travel. Following an increase of 5 percent in revenue sales in less than six months, the services were furnished to the other half of the internal agents and to the 18,000 external independent agents.

SOA enabled faster interaction of the internal and external agents with best-of-class external airline, cruise, government, insurance, and rail organizations that partner with firms in the leisure and travel industry. The information technology department integrated an identification process for transactions of travelers in eXtensible Markup Language (XML) or SOAP, in an effort to expedite processing of the transactions with external partners. These organizations were participants in Open Travel Alliance (OTA) XML standards of the industry.

SOA was not extended to having personalized planning on the Web. However, with an expanding culture of education and of innovation in the marketing department, planning by travelers on the Web was expected in 2007 in an incremental strategy. The information technology department learned from failure in the original SOA project. The department was educated on the management of services in an SOA and instituted an enterprise architecture and governance group on SOA. Services were no longer managed by the consultant team. Finally, Microsoft and Oracle were the technologies of the SOA in the study.

Program Management Methodology: Overview

The program management methodology enabled the new project with an effective incremental solution of SOA. Figure 3.9 depicts the methodology frameworks for Case Study 5, while Table 3.9 provides the key factors for this case study.

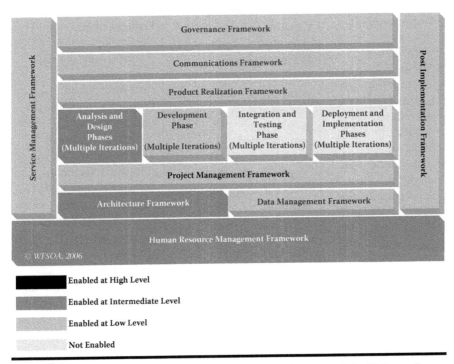

Figure 3.9 Methodology frameworks for Case Study 5: travel and leisure firm.

Table 3.9 Key Factors for Case Study 5

Business Factors	Procedural Factors	Technical Factors
Agility, efficiency, and flexibility benefits Financial benefits Competitive, market, and regulatory differentials Customer demand Organizational change management Executive sponsorship Executive technology leadership Focus on improvement of process Service orientation Reusability of assets	Control of program SOA center of competency Responsibilities and roles Education and training Knowledge exchange Change management Information management Common reference Technology firm knowledge capture Risk management Standards management Infrastructure architecture Process and service deployment environment Process and service deployment techniques Service management and support Security management Continuous process improvement Costing techniques Strategy management	Internal SOA domain on project External process domain on project External SOA domain on project Business process management product software Middleware Platform of key technology firms Platform specialty tools from platform technology firm Proprietary technologies XML standard Messaging standards Service description and discovery standards Transaction standards Security standards User interface standards Web services best practices Web services management standards

Governance

The project was enabled by governance at a low level, due to the lack of service catalog management and limited executive business leadership, so important in the management of services.

For the project, factors of control of program, executive technology leadership, and executive sponsorship, in educating and empowering agents on Web-based functionality, were evident however in the focus on incremental strategy. Documentation and knowledge exchange from the consulting firm to the information technology department in process and service deployment environment as well as process and service deployment techniques were evident in the eventual knowledge of the department. Standards management in transaction and security management, and limited strategy management, were evident later in the project. Focus on improvement of process and continuous process improvement were evident as goals of senior management.

Risk management was evident as a factor in governance.

Communications

The project was enabled by communications at a low level.

Agility, efficiency, and flexibility benefits; financial benefits; competitive, market, and regulatory differentials; customer demand; and organizational change management were evident as goals of the new project. Knowledge exchange on SOA was evident, however, later in the project. Common reference was evident in the synchronization of services with OTA schema standards.

Although these factors were evident in communications, the factor of executive business leadership on a promotion of the program and the strategy was not as evident on the project.

Product Realization

The project was enabled by product realization at a generally low level, as the phase of development was low with business process management software and phases of integration and testing and deployment and implementation were not evident on the project.

Responsibilities and roles were evident, however, in the mandate of a new Chief Information Officer (CIO) who required an SOA technology department, and technology firm knowledge capture from the consulting and technology firms was evident later in product realization.

This project included external process domain.

Project Management

The project was enabled by project management at a low level, as the project was managed by the technology firms, which were not supervised by the business firm in the study.

Architecture

The project was enabled by architecture at an intermediate level, as the project was in the beginning of evolution in SOA.

Infrastructure architecture was evident, however, in the best features of heterogeneous internal agent applications and of the external agent and organization proprietary applications, which were integrated in an interface for all agents and all organizations partnered with the firm. More than 100 features were integrated into the interface on a portal as shared services. Service description and discovery standards included WSDL for descriptions, the XML standard for exchange of information, and SOAP for messaging standards. Middleware was included on caching on an ESB (enterprise service bus). Infrastructure included internal SOA domains and external SOA domains, with platform of key technology firms, platform specialty tools from platform technology firm, and limited proprietary technologies.

Transaction standards and security standards and Web services best practices and Web services management standards were evident on the project.

Data Management

The project was enabled by data management at a low level, in information management in caching customized destination packaging, itinerary planning and pricing for data mining, but not in improving data.

Service Management

The project was enabled by service management at a low level, due to lack of integration of the business staff with the technical staff.

Factors of focus on improvement of process, reusability of assets and service orientation, and change management in guidance of the new project were evident with the technical staff, but not with the business staff.

User interface standards were helpful in service management but were limited on the project.

Human Resource Management

The project was enabled by human resource management at an intermediate level.

Education and training in 21st century business and consumer practices of travel with the Web were evident in attempting to improve the culture in the firm. The impact of services on the industry was included in the training. Training was for both the technical staff and the business agent and marketing staff. The technical staff was further trained on service-oriented technology. This training was evident finally in an SOA center of competency team that focused on "best practice" reusability of services.

Responsibilities and roles of a new technology department were not finalized from the product realization framework of the project, thus impacting the enablement of the human resource framework.

Post Implementation

The project was enabled by post implementation in service management and support, security management, and costing techniques, but at a low level, inasmuch as service level agreements (SLAs) were not formalized in the firm.

Key Program Roles

Table 3.10 provides the key program roles for Case Study 5.

Table 3.10   Key Program Roles for Case Study 5

Corporate Sector Executive sponsor Personnel specialist Training specialist
Business Sector Business manager Business analyst for extended organization
Governance Sector SOA strategist Technology knowledge specialist
Technology Sector Security specialist Infrastructure architect Database administrator

Summary of Project

The project in Case Study 5 is an example of an emerging external and internal incremental SOA solution in which governance, project management, and service management may have to be expanded for new services to ensure a successful SOA strategy.

Key Lessons Learned on Project

- Competitive differential of a firm is not forever in an industry, as a firm must be diligent in ensuring an edge in its industry.
- Culture of innovation in a large-sized firm contributes to potential receptivity to SOA.
- Education and training of business staff on the impact of SOA and of technical staff on the management of SOA contribute critically in SOA solutions and strategy.

Maturity of SOA on Project

Figure 3.10 illustrates the maturity of SOA for the Case Study 5 project.

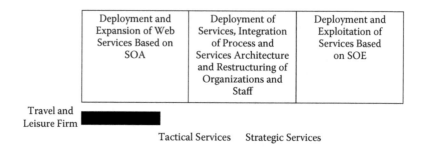

Figure 3.10 Maturity of SOA for Case Study 5 project.

Chapter 4 discusses deployment of services, integration of process and services architecture, and potential restructuring of organizations and staff.

Chapter 4

Deployment of Services, Integration of Process and Services Architecture, and Restructuring of Organizations and Staff

This chapter discusses the deployment of services, the integration of process and services architecture, and potentially restructuring organizations and staff in a broadband communications firm (Case Study 6), a certification testing firm (Case Study 7), an investment advisory firm (Case Study 8), an insurance firm (Case Study 9), a municipal energy utility (Case Study 10), a banking firm (Case Study 11), a telecommunications firm (Case Study 12), and a software firm (Case Study 13).

Case Study 6: Broadband Communications Firm

Core Project: Internal Business Unit Process

Background of Firm

The firm in Case Study 6 consisted of a broadband communications business with a breadth of products marketed from 100+ offices in different markets. This firm was a leader in its industry in the deployment of Web services and SOA to compete in a demanding and changing marketplace. The information technology (IT) department had deployed numerous component services by 2006 that contributed to efficiency gains of 500 percent in a number of the firm's business units. Although services contributed tangible improvement in current product processes of the units, they were not coordinated by the firm for either current or future business in the industry. The firm did not have effective governance of the design, development, integration, and deployment of services for its business.

Business Challenge

The original services in this study, as in the processes in the other studies, were generally inefficient and non-agile for the enterprise of the firm. Although the technology department had a committee for governance, the committee emphasized continued deployment of services for the business units, without control and without a focus on critical deployment for the firm. Because of this condition, different sections of the technology department deployed duplicate and inconsistent services in diverse sections of the units. Estimates indicated that 20 percent of the $100+ million budget of the technology department was for redundant processing scenarios of SOA. Reusability of services and of software was not evident in this study.

The firm had to deploy *efficient* enterprise *services* so that there would be less cost and redundancy in existent services and in future services, and *agile services* so that there would be "on-demand" reusability of services and software without hindering fast deployment for demands of the marketplace and of the business units.

This firm had to have formal governance of independent rogue services that could be reused by the business.

Deployment of Services

The focus of this project was to control the services in the business units, cut the costs of the services, and have an efficient and agile SOA. The solution was an SOA with formal governance of services in the firm. This solution was enabled by investment in centralized catalog management.

The IT department educated the business units in the criticality of formal governance of services, with the help of the Chief Executive Officer (CEO) of the firm who concurred in the objectives of the project. Upon concurrence of the business units, the technology department invested in a Universal Description, Discovery and Integration (UDDI) registry and repository system from Hewlett-Packard (Systinet) for control of metadata and parameters of the services. Because the business staff in the units had already defined the processes and the services, the staff in the technology department had to learn the business nomenclature of these processes and services to insert them into the system.

Case Study 6: Pre-SOA

Broadband Communications Firm							
Business Unit 1			Business Unit 2			Business Unit 3	
Department 1			Department 2	Department 3		Department 4	
Service 1A	Service 1B**	Service 2C	Service 3A	Service 3B**	Service 4A	Service 5A	Service 5B**

Case Study 6: SOA

Broadband Communications Firm					
Business Unit 1		Business Unit 2			Business Unit 3
Service 1A***	Service 2C	Service 3A***	Service 4A***	Service 5A***	Service 6D*

* Additional Service
** Duplicate Services of Existing Services
*** Shared Services

Figure 4.1 Reusability of services in Case Study 6.

Once the services of the units were included in the registry of the system, redundancy of the services was obvious to both the technical staff and the business staff on the project. Redundancy of the services was estimated 30 percent. Reusability of the decentralized services was eventually facilitated by having the same terminology in the centralized system and is illustrated in Figure 4.1.

Reusability was managed with AmberPoint service management technology. Although the foremost goal of the project was control of services in the business units, the registry and repository system was an enabling foundation for the governance of SOA in the enterprise firm.

Program Management Methodology: Overview

The program management methodology enabled the project with effective governance and service management solutions of SOA. Figure 4.2 illustrates the methodology frameworks for Case Study 6, and Table 4.1 presents the key factors for this case study.

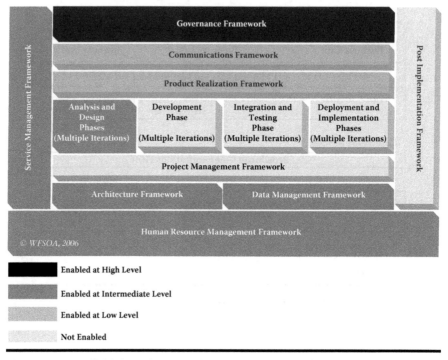

Figure 4.2   Methodology frameworks for Case Study 6: broadband communications firm.

Table 4.1 Key Factors for Case Study 6

Business Factors	Procedural Factors	Technical Factors
Agility, efficiency, and flexibility benefits	Control of program	Internal SOA domain on project
Financial benefits	Responsibilities and roles	Business process management product software
Business client participation	Education and training	
Culture of innovation	Knowledge exchange	Middleware
Executive technology leadership	Change management	Platform of key technology firms
Strategic planning	Information management	
Enterprise architecture	Common reference	Proprietary technologies
Focus on improvement of process	Naming conventions	Best-of-class tools
Service orientation	Procurement of technology	Service description and discovery standards
Reusability of assets	Risk management	
	Standards management	
	Infrastructure architecture	
	Process and service deployment environment	
	Process and service deployment techniques	
	Service catalog management	
	Service management and support	
	Security management	

Note: Definitions of *factors* are in Table 2.2 in Chapter 2 and may be referenced in more than one framework.

Methodology Frameworks and Key Factor Highlights on Project

Governance

The project was enabled by governance at a high level.

Factors of control of program of the project and eventual strategic planning of the business units of the firm were highly evident in the concurrence of the business units in centralized governance of decentralized services, to ensure agility, efficiency, and flexibility benefits and financial benefits. Education and training of the technical staff and the business staff were evident in the eventual evolution of governance of information technology to governance of SOA. Enterprise architecture, common reference, and infrastructure architecture were facilitated by the evolution.

Business process management product software with Business Process Execution Language (BPEL) standards was evident in the control of the process and service deployment environment of the services.

Service orientation, knowledge exchange, and service catalog management were evident in the concurrence of business and technical staff on the new committee of governance to evaluate future services for inclusion in the production registry system. Services had to have business objectives and metadata in service description and discovery standards (UDDI). Services were not to be included in the system without an evaluation by the committee.

Service management and support software and standards management of the technology were evident on the project.

Software technology of Hewlett-Packard and AmberPoint was evaluated as best-of-class tools in procurement of technology and risk management procedures on the project.

Communications

The project was enabled and helped by communications at a low level, in factors of business client participation, culture of innovation, and executive technology leadership, and common reference and naming conventions were evident in terminology.

Further communications by the CEO in executive sponsorship or executive business leadership on the importance of SOA were not evident on the project.

Product Realization

The project was enabled by product realization in the registry and repository systems and in the scorecard tools furnished by the process and service deployment techniques of the platforms of Hewlett-Packard and AmberPoint and of limited proprietary technologies, but this framework was essentially at a low level, as development, integration and testing, and deployment and implementation phases were not evident in the study.

The project was enabled, however, by extreme programming (XP) project management, in the prototyping of process and service deployment techniques.

This project included internal SOA domain.

Project Management

The project was not enabled by formal project management.

Architecture

The project was enabled by architecture at an intermediate level, in middleware, and notably in security management, but was not fully implemented in an SOA strategy.

Data Management

The project was enabled by data management at an intermediate level, in the information management of the database behind the data catalog registry system, but was not fully implemented with a data model external to the registry system.

Service Management

The project was enabled by service management at an intermediate level, in focus on improvement of process, reusability of assets, change management, and introduction of service catalog management, for the enterprise of the firm, but was informal in methodology.

Human Resource Management

The project was enabled by human resource management at an intermediate level, due to the lack of an organizational change management program.

New responsibilities and roles of the technical staff and the business staff were evident on the committee of governance, but not evident was the initiation of an SOA center of competency for integration of key technical staff in the diverse sections of the technology department.

Post Implementation

The project was not enabled by post implementation, due to limited organizational restructuring.

Key Program Roles

Table 4.2 presents the key program roles in Case Study 6.

**Table 4.2   Key Program Roles
for Case Study 6**

Corporate Sector Training specialist
Business Sector Business analyst Business process project specialist
Governance Sector SOA program coordinator Service librarian Communications coordinator
Technology Sector Technical sponsor Security specialist Database analyst Service manager

Summary of Project

The project in Case Study 6 is an example of a first-mover firm that invested in services in diverse business units without the enterprise functions of governance to manage the services in an SOA strategy.

Key Lessons Learned on Project

- Enterprise governance of services can contribute to cost-efficient and agile SOA solutions.
- Focus on reusability of services can contribute to a prudent SOA strategy.

Maturity of SOA on Project

Figure 4.3 reveals the maturity of SOA on the Case Study 6 project.

Deployment and Expansion of Web Services Based on SOA	Deployment of Services, Integration of Process and Services Architecture and Restructuring of Organizations and Staff	Deployment and Exploitation of Services Based on SOE

Broadband Communications Firm

Tactical Services   Strategic Services

Figure 4.3   Maturity of SOA for the Case Study 6 project.

Case Study 7: Certification Testing Firm

Core Project: Internal Business Unit Process

Background of Firm

The firm in Case Study 7 consisted of a certification testing business for 7+ million academic, corporate, and governmental customers. The firm delivered standardized testing in 3,000+ offices in 110+ countries and on the Web. Tests were delivered by instructors in 20+ languages. This firm grew its business by acquiring numerous other testing firms that had their own customer databases and customized registration, scheduling, and testing applications. The firm had to maintain the process of certification testing, which included the applications of the acquired businesses and of the central business.

Business Challenge

The process was costly and inefficient for the firm because the acquired firms furnished diverse formats of questions and answers from tests to be input into the central application of the firm, which was not as fast for customers as in other certification firms in the industry. The acquired firms had multiple platforms and proprietary technologies behind the applications. Forcing the firms into a single platform of the firm was not feasible, and enterprise application integration (EAI) of a few of the nonproprietary applications was not helpful, as the firms had a substantial investment in their platforms and their applications.

The process was inflexible, as changes to the applications due to privacy regulation and security in the international offices had to be individually integrated into the applications, to avoid being fined by regulatory organizations. The process was not agile for this growing firm, as new offerings of tests had to be integrated into the individualized applications and synchronized throughout the offices. The deployment of tests was not as fast as in other firms in the testing industry.

The firm in this study had to deploy an *agile* and competitive *process* so that there would be faster deployment of new offerings of tests, a *flexible process* so that there would be faster inclusion of regulatory and security requirements, and an *efficient process* so that the specialized applications of the acquired firms would be integrated for faster processing of results of tests.

Deployment of Services

The focus of the project was to deploy immediately a solution of SOA to effectively integrate the processing of registration, scheduling, and testing in the full firm.

The technology department of the firm first defined the business logic of the certification testing business in business process management (BPM) product software.

The department divided the processing requirements of the business into composite services consisting of component granular services of an SOA. The firm invested in an XML gateway that helped in integrating the information in the individualized applications of the firms into the central home office application. The gateway facilitated integration of new offerings of tests and regulatory and security requirements without recoding the applications. Information transformation and request routing of tests were furnished by the gateway for all the applications in the full firm.

The firm invested in performance monitoring to ensure faster processing of the business with SOA.

SOA is estimated to have saved $1.5+ million in operations of the full firm in 2006, with $10+ million forecasted savings in 2008.

SOA included BPM Microsoft technology, the gateway networking and security technology of Reactivity, and the performance monitoring tools of Progress Software (Actional).

Program Management Methodology: Overview

The program management methodology enabled and helped this project with an effective SOA solution. Figure 4.4 presents the methodology frameworks for Case Study 7, and Table 4.3 provides the key factors for this case study.

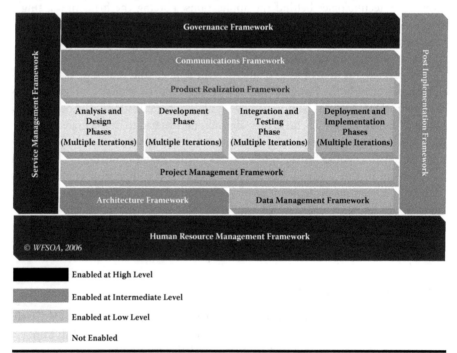

Figure 4.4   Methodology frameworks for Case Study 7: certification testing firm.

Table 4.3 Key Factors for Case Study 7

Business Factors	Procedural Factors	Technical Factors
Agility, efficiency, and flexibility benefits	Control of program	Internal SOA domain on project
Financial benefits	SOA center of competency	External SOA domain on project
Business client participation	Responsibilities and roles	Business process management product software
Competitive, market, and regulatory differentials	Education and training	
	Knowledge exchange	
	Change management	
Customer demand	Information management	Data tools
Culture of innovation	Common reference	Middleware
Organizational change management	Naming conventions	Platform of key technology firms
	Procurement of technology	Platform specialty tools from platform technology firm
Executive sponsorship	Risk management	
Executive technology leadership	Standards management	Best-of-class tools
	Infrastructure architecture	XML standard
Strategic planning	Process and service deployment techniques	Messaging standards
Focus on improvement of process	Service management and support	Transaction standards
Service orientation		Security standards
Reusability of assets	Security management	

Governance

The project was enabled by governance at a high level.

Factors of service orientation and business process management products were evident in the focus on improvement of business process and services, not technical services, at the beginning of the project. Control of program was evident in the strategic planning of the project for agility, efficiency, and flexibility benefits, and financial benefits. Competitive, market, and regulatory differentials and customer demand were factors in the planning. Control of program was evident in enforced reusability of assets, naming conventions, and standards management, so that services would be accessible by the home office of the firm. Responsibilities and roles of defined technical and business staff in the firms and in the home office of the firm were evident in organizational change management on the project.

Risk management, service management and support, and security standards were evident on the project.

Procurement of technology, data tools, and best-of-class tools were evident on the project.

SOA center of competency was eventually initiated in the home office of the firm.

Communications

The project was enabled by communications at an intermediate level, in business client participation, knowledge exchange, and common reference, which furnished consistent business, process, service, and technical terminology in the firm.

Executive technology leadership with executive sponsorship was helpful in communications, but executive business leadership was minimal to nonexistent on the project.

Product Realization

The project was enabled by product realization at a low level, due to a focus on an immediate registration, scheduling, and testing solution initiated in the deployment and implementation phases without integration and testing, development or design and analysis phases.

This project included internal SOA domain and external SOA domain with process and service deployment techniques.

Project Management

The project was enabled by formal project management at a low level, except for follow-up by senior management in the firm's home office.

Architecture

The project was enabled by architecture at an intermediate level, in common infrastructure architecture for the interoperability of external registration, scheduling, and testing applications and in security management, middleware, XML standard, messaging standards, transaction standards, and security standards of the external applications.

Platform of key technology firms and platform specialty tools from platform technology firms were evident on the project.

Not evident was infrastructure architecture in integrating internal applications on the project.

Data Management

The project was enabled by a data-centric methodology to SOA in the design of flows of processes around common definitions of XML schema for the full firm and not around isolated data representations of applications of the firms, which was evident in information management, but was informal at a low level, due to the focus on external applications and not integration of internal applications of the firm.

Service Management

The project was enabled by a focus on service management at a high level in change management in the evaluation of the processes and the required services for the full firm, which was highly important in the implementation of services in this study.

Human Resource Management

The project was enabled by human resource management at a high level in the culture of innovation and education and training of the technical and business staff in the home office of the firm and of designated staff of the other firms.

Post Implementation

The project was enabled by post implementation at an intermediate level, in the monitoring of performance of the deployed services with best-of-class tools.

Not evident immediately was an SOA center of competency, the purpose of which was to formalize education and training in the firm, although the center was gradually initiated later in governance and post implementation.

Key Program Roles

Table 4.4 presents the key program roles for Case Study 7.

Table 4.4   Key Program Roles for Case Study 7

Corporate Sector Executive sponsor
Business Sector Business sponsor
Governance Sector Technology transfer specialist Communications specialist Process specialist
Technology Sector Technical sponsor Database analyst Security specialist Infrastructure architect SOA developer

Summary of Project

The project in Case Study 7 is an example of a firm that had to deploy a service solution, due to the continued growth of its business from acquired firms, and deployed a solution with a generally effective governance and information management methodology.

Key Lessons Learned on Project

- Acquisitions of diverse firms and inherited applications can contribute to the adoption of SOA.
- Gateways can contribute to the fast deployment of SOA.
- Implementation of common referencing and naming conventions can contribute to the enablement of SOA.
- Information management contributes to the critical enablement of SOA.
- Integration of performance monitoring technology helps in post implementation of SOA.

Maturity of SOA on Project

Figure 4.5 illustrates the maturity of SOA for the Case Study 7 project.

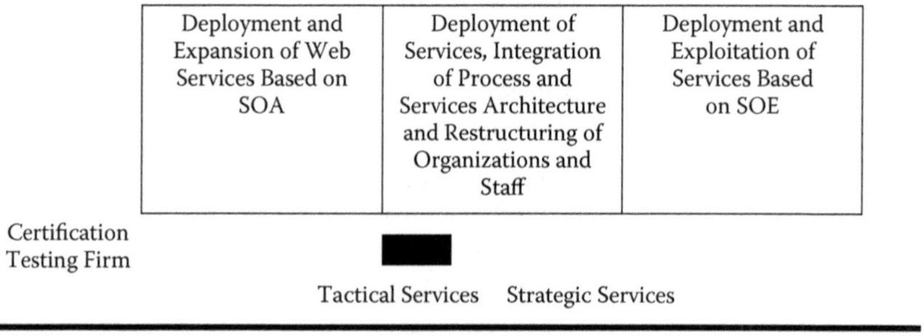

Deployment and Expansion of Web Services Based on SOA	Deployment of Services, Integration of Process and Services Architecture and Restructuring of Organizations and Staff	Deployment and Exploitation of Services Based on SOE

Certification Testing Firm

Tactical Services   Strategic Services

Figure 4.5   Maturity of SOA for Case Study 7 project.

Case Study 8: Investment Advisory Firm

Core Project: Internal Business Unit Process

Background of Firm

The firm in Case Study 8 consisted of an investment advisory institution. The function of the institution was to direct the financial assets of high-income customers and corporate institutions and to handle a daily 1.5+ million customer service requests and $250+ billion securities trades. The firm had 85+ domestic and 5+ international locations.

The concern of executive management was that competitor firms were furnishing customer self-service Web sites and systems. This firm had customer care representatives who answered calls on the telephone from corporate institutions and customers on account balancing, benefit checks, custody holdings, fund transfers, and income tax forms. The customers included 20 percent of the highest net income consumers in the country, and they were consistently demanding online self-service solutions.

Domestic customer care representatives, who had to be fully knowledgeable of the customer holdings and the firm's financial products, had to maintain the process of interfacing with the customers.

Business Challenge

This process was neither agile nor flexible for a firm in this industry. Customer inquiry on the telephone and not on the Web was costly because of the dependence on the customer care representatives. Customized investment analysis could not be done by customers on the Web without deployed functionality, while analysis could be done on competitor Web sites with different investment planning tools. Service was not 24/7. Service was not flexible to handle increased inquires during product promotion periods.

Information for the customer care representatives came from desktop displays connected to client/server and legacy applications. Information on account holdings and products of customers and corporate institutions was not current on these displays because of delays in processing telephoned transactions into the applications. Information was flawed due to errors on product securities trades, because of offline processing of the trades into diverse applications.

This firm had to deploy a *flexible process* so that there would be current customer and institution information for the representatives and faster response to customers and institutions during peak periods, and an *agile process* so that there would be self-service for customers as with competitors. Flexibility and agility in helping high-income customers and institutions were critical for a best-of-class investment advisory institution.

Deployment of Services

The focus of the project in this firm was to have a flexible and agile process for improved interaction with customers and institutions. The solution in this study was an SOA that empowered institutions and customers with customized and personalized portals on the Web. Portals were designed externally for distinct groups of high-income customers and corporate institutions for access to account holdings and product promotions independent of customer care representatives. Features included financial planning tools. Portals were designed internally for representatives to help customers who contacted the representatives on the telephone or on the Web, and interaction with customers decreased from minutes to seconds as fundamental functions were available on the external portals. This solution contributed to faster 24/7 availability of information for institutions and individual customers.

SOA integrated functions of legacy applications of the firm into interfaces on the portals. Functions from 30+ legacy applications, including custody holding management, cash management, and asset management, merged into interfaces of component services in less than six months, with some of services available in a shorter period. Errors from institutions and customers and from representatives were generally eliminated in the SOA due to online processing of trades. Impact in improved interaction and knowledge of the representatives was evident in increased retention and satisfaction of customers and institutions. SOA included BEA Web-Logic consulting and technology for inclusion of the services into the interfaces of the portals, Microsoft .NET for customized development of the interfaces to the applications, and Oracle (Oblix) for security of the services.

Flexibility and agility in faster information and self-service enabled in the SOA contributed to a designation of the firm as an innovator in an *Information Week* 500 Survey in 2006.

Program Management Methodology: Overview

The program management methodology enabled the project in this study with an effective and fast solution of SOA. Figure 4.6 shows the methodology frameworks for Case Study 8, and Table 4.5 provides the key factors for this case study.

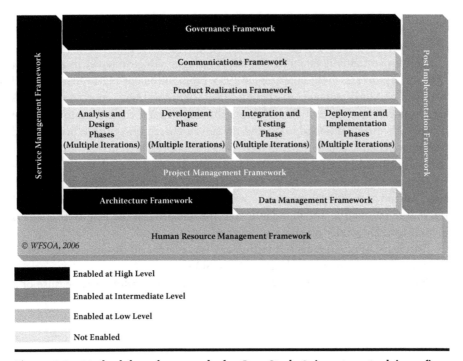

Figure 4.6 Methodology frameworks for Case Study 8: investment advisory firm.

Table 4.5 Key Factors for Case Study 8

Business Factors	Procedural Factors	Technical Factors
Agility, efficiency, and flexibility benefits	Control of program	Internal Web services on project
Business client participation	Change management	External SOA domain on project
Competitive, market, and regulatory differentials	Procurement of technology	Business process management product software
Customer demand	Risk management	Platform of key technology firms
Culture of innovation	Infrastructure architecture	Platform specialty tools from platform technology firm
Executive business leadership	Process and service deployment techniques	XML standard
Executive technology leadership	Service catalog management	Messaging standards
Strategic planning	Service management and support	Service description and discovery standards
Focus on improvement of process	Security management	Security standards
Service orientation	Continuous process improvement	Web services best practices
Reusability of assets	Strategy management	

Governance

The project was enabled by governance at a high level.

This firm essentially established control of program in governance in a blueprint of business processes in the enterprise in 1995. From the blueprint, the firm deployed Web services consistent with an existing culture of innovation, a continuous process improvement strategy, and an evolving technology, in a focus on improvement of process. The firm continued to expand the services based on agility, efficiency, and flexibility benefits; competitive, market, and regulatory differentials; and customer demand planned in the strategy. Deployment was initiated in internal functionality but external functionality for customers was not initiated until this project. External functionality for customers was enabled, however, by the foundation of internal functionality. The foundation and the blueprint of the firm were enablers of an inherently service orientation strategy.

The factor of procurement of technology was evident on the project because of an enterprise evaluation of technology in an SOA.

Not evident on the project was the factor of costing techniques, because of a higher focus on functionality than on savings.

Communications

The project was not as enabled by communications as by governance, inasmuch as the interaction of the consulting staff with the technical and business staff in the firm was not evident in the study.

Product Realization

The project was not enabled by formal phases of analysis and design, development, integration and testing, and deployment and implementation in the external SOA domain of the study.

Project Management

The project was essentially enabled at an intermediate level, with executive business leadership in the business operations department and executive technology leadership in the information technology department, which were evident as factors on the project.

The project initiated with the consulting firm, which instituted an initial project management organization, to implement SOA, but the organization was at an intermediate level of maturity.

Architecture

The project was enabled by architecture at a high level.

SOA was enabled by a foundation of services since 1995.

Factors of infrastructure architecture, risk management, process and service deployment techniques, security management, internal Web services, platform of key technology firm, platform specialty tools from platform technology firm, XML standard, messaging standards, service description and discovery standards, security standards, and Web services best practices were evident on the project, as on projects of first-mover firms in SOA.

Data Management

The project was not as enabled by data management as by architecture, as the data in the existing legacy applications was largely linked into the new portals without further investigation of the data.

Service Management

The project was enabled by service management at a high level because decisions on delivery of services were based on the blueprint of business processes in the enterprise, which was cited in the framework of governance.

Factors of change management, service catalog management, service management and support, and strategy management and business process management product software were evident on the project, and business client participation was helpful on the project.

Goals included reusability of assets in the firm.

Human Resource Management

The project was enabled at a low level due to lack of inclusion of internal staff.

Not evident fully on the project was technology firm knowledge capture.

Post Implementation

The project was enabled by post implementation at an intermediate level due to the lack of service level agreements (SLAs) and service monitoring reviews.

Key Program Roles

Table 4.6 presents the key program roles for Case Study 8.

**Table 4.6   Key Program Roles
for Case Study 8**

Corporate Sector
Executive sponsor

Governance Sector
SOA strategist
SOA program coordinator
Program methodology specialist
Process specialist

Technology Sector
Infrastructure architect

Summary of Project

Although governance, project management, architecture, service management, human resource management, and post implementation enabled the project, Case Study 8 is an example of a departmental SOA solution that, because of enterprise architecture, can be expanded in future processes and services. Existing governance can help in the expansion. Communications, product realization, project management, and data management may have to be expanded to have fewer external consultants and more internal technology staff, to ensure a controlled and managed path of a successful SOA strategy.

Key Lessons Learned on Project

- Definition of a blueprint can contribute to enterprise service-oriented architecture, and service management can expand service solutions.
- Evolution of functionality on incremental projects, in contrast to "big bang" projects, can be an effective SOA strategy.
- Integration of portal technology can facilitate solutions and strategy.

Maturity of SOA on Project

Figure 4.7 illustrates the maturity of SOA for the Case Study 8 project.

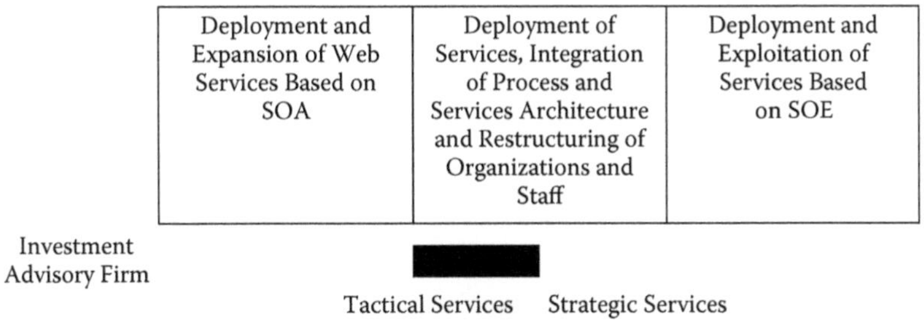

Deployment and Expansion of Web Services Based on SOA	Deployment of Services, Integration of Process and Services Architecture and Restructuring of Organizations and Staff	Deployment and Exploitation of Services Based on SOE

Investment Advisory Firm ████████

Tactical Services   Strategic Services

Figure 4.7   Maturity of SOA for Case Study 8 project.

Case Study 9: Insurance Firm

Core Project: Internal Firm Process Integration

Background of Firm

The firm in this case study consisted of an established second-tier insurance business. This firm furnished auto and business insurance and personal life policy products to customers. Independent agents marketed the products to the customers in a national network, based on different applications from customer relationship management (CRM) to enterprise resource planning (ERP). Features and information in the applications were enhanced for availability by the agents in an early and frequent deployment of services. The firm had a goal to become a first-tier business by expanding Web services.

The executives in the business units of the firm however had a concern that the agent applications were becoming complex and costly. They had a concurrent concern that the applications were not customizable for agent demand or for competitive differential of the firm, despite expansion of services in the firm. Because of these concerns, managers were hesitant about future investment in services but they still had the goal of becoming a first-tier business.

The issue in this study was that the firm focused on departmental projects of Web services that were not in tandem with an enterprise architecture platform of an SOA to integrate the services.

Business Challenge

This insurance firm had legacy applications dating back to 1965. The functions and the information in the applications were available in complex and numerous Web services, which were controlled in the departments of the firm but centrally funded by the information technology department. Although functionality and information are advantageous for departmental units when contained in services rather than in legacy applications, the costs of maintenance of customized distributed services are higher than maintenance of centrally controlled services, governed in an enterprise architecture platform of an SOA.

The costs of potentially redundant Web services would continue to be higher, and customization of functionality and information would continue to be inflexible, in the continued expansion of projects of services without enterprise architecture of an SOA. The firm would not be a first-tier business in the insurance industry without an enterprise architecture platform.

This firm had to deploy a *flexible process* so that the agents would have functionality and information from enterprise services at their fingertips.

Deployment of Services

The focus of the project was to cut the costs of information technology in the firm but furnish customizable information to the independent agents. The solution was a pilot project for "on-demand" multi-quote services in a structured SOA. This solution was deployable for the internal employees and managers as well as external independent agents.

SOA furnished enterprise component services that helped the agents classify customers and discern insurance risks. The services were expanded for further information in customizable composite services accessible in a centrally managed Web-based portal. Services linked to the legacy applications of departments and business units that had the information as in Figure 4.8. The technology department developed and integrated the platform reference architecture behind the services from a design of the enterprise, not from conditions or a design of a business unit or a department in the firm. Information integrated in the pilot project of the SOA, and in subsequent projects in 2005, was a competitive differential for the independent agents and managers of the firm.

SOA included BEA WebLogic, IBM WebSphere, and Oracle ERP technologies in this study.

SOA saved 10 percent or $15+ million in the costs of the information technology department in 2005, from less redundancy of services. Evolution to SOA convinced executives in this firm of the importance of an enterprise architecture platform and of service management in a first-tier strategy. This firm is forecasting first-tier status in 2007.

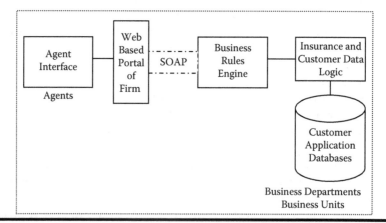

Figure 4.8 Services linked to legacy applications in Case Study 9.

Program Management Methodology: Overview

The program management methodology enabled the project with an effective evolutionary solution of SOA with existing technology firms. Figure 4.9 illustrates the methodology frameworks for Case Study 9, and Table 4.7 provides the key factors evident in this case study.

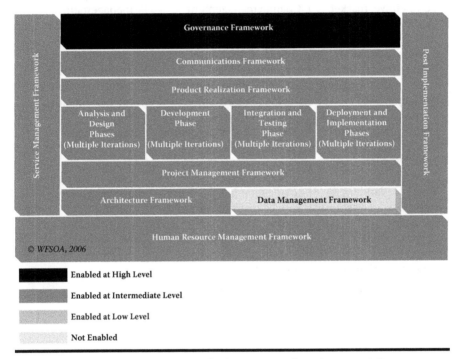

Figure 4.9 Methodology frameworks for Case Study 9: insurance firm.

Table 4.7   Key Factors for Case Study 9

Business Factors	Procedural Factors	Technical Factors
Agility, efficiency, and flexibility benefits Financial benefits Business client participation Competitive, market, and regulatory differentials Customer demand Culture of innovation Organizational change management Executive sponsorship Executive business leadership Executive technology leadership Strategic planning Enterprise architecture Focus on improvement of process Service orientation Reusability of assets	Control of program SOA center of competency Responsibilities and roles Education and training Knowledge exchange Change management Procurement of technology Technology firm knowledge capture Risk management Standards management Infrastructure architecture Process and service deployment environment Process and service deployment techniques Service catalog management Service management and support Security management Continuous process improvement Strategy management	Internal SOA domain on project External SOA domain on project Business process management product software Platform of key technology firms Platform specialty tools from platform technology firm Proprietary technologies XML standard Messaging standards Service description and discovery standards Security standards Web services best practices

Governance

The project was enabled by governance at a high level, as evident in executive sponsorship and strategic planning, and also in enterprise architecture and strategy management.

The factor of control of program directed by the enterprise architecture group of the firm was highly evident on the project. This group in the information technology department focused on factors of agility, efficiency, and flexibility benefits; competitive, market, and regulatory differentials; and customer demand that conformed to strategic planning. Financial benefits from the foundation of an SOA were a further factor evident in the project. Focus on improvement of process and service orientation was highly evident in the project, as implied in Figure 4.8. Service catalog management and service management and support enabled control of culture of innovation and service orientation.

The technology department customized the Capability Maturity Model Integration (CMMI) methodology with a consulting firm on the project, to expand the continuous process improvement of SOA. Customization consisted of deployment of basic services of SOA at the initial level of CMMI, component services at the managed level, and integration of enterprise architecture at the defined level of CMMI. Factors of organizational change management, infrastructure architecture, security management, risk management, and strategy management were evident in the methodology on the project. Formalization and integration of process and service deployment environment, and process and service deployment techniques facilitated Web services best practices with standards and tools. Knowledge exchange from the consultants was evident and helped the technology staff.

Executive business leadership, executive technology leadership, and executive sponsorship were evident in the firm in the evolution of the project into 2007.

Communications

The project was enabled by communications at an intermediate level in knowledge exchange of the technology department to the business units on the importance of a controlled but distributed SOA, in contrast to distributed but isolated and redundant Web services.

Further communications on common reference of terminology was not evident however, and it was important to have in the comprehension and consolidation of applications on this project.

Product Realization

The project was enabled by product realization at an intermediate level.

Process and service deployment environment facilitated knowledge exchange in the technology department and technology firm knowledge capture. Best practices in design, development, integration, testing, and deployment were evident in the evolutionary SOA. Reusability of assets was evident on the project.

Further evidence, however, of formal integration of the phases of product realization was needed on the project.

This project included internal SOA domain and external SOA domain.

Project Management

The project was enabled by project management at an intermediate level, in focus on improvement of process, and executive business leadership and executive technology leadership were evident factors on the project, but otherwise the project was not enabled by formal methodology.

Architecture

The project was enabled by architecture at an intermediate level, due to more focus on external applications than on internal applications.

The enterprise architecture group of the technology department focused on enterprise architecture strategy. The lack of standards on the previous Web services necessitated standards management, business process management products, XML standard, messaging standards (SOAP), service description and discovery standards (UDDI), and security standards (Web Services-Security Policy [WS-SP]). The procurement of technology ensured standards were evident in the platform of key technology firms, the platform specialty tools from platform technology firms, and the proprietary software technologies.

SOA center of competency was evident on the project, but with limited indication of responsibilities and roles of staff.

Data Management

The project was not as enabled by information management as by the other frameworks of the methodology on the project. Data was neither mapped nor normalized across the applications of the firm. Further focus on information management will enable an improved SOA.

Service Management

The project was enabled by service management at an intermediate level in the mandate given to the enterprise architecture group to control change management processes, but the business staff deferred to the technical staff.

The project manager in the group controlled a registry of applications, data, external and internal services, and technologies. The group decided projects on conformance to strategic planning and to the enterprise architecture of the firm. This group demonstrated the benefits of centralized and controlled ownership of services. Business client participation in requirements of services was important on the project.

Human Resource Management

The project was enabled by human resource management at an intermediate level, in extensive education and training of the developer groups of the technology department, initiated by an introduced SOA center of competency. Development staff was hesitant in moving to an environment not developed but composed of services. Training was important in shifting the paradigm to the potential of reusability of services.

Further focus on formal responsibilities and roles of the technical staff, with the maturity of the SOA center of competency, was expected following the results of the training.

Post Implementation

The project was enabled by post implementation at an intermediate level due to the improvement needed in the management of "on-demand" services and in security management.

Further inclusion of responsibilities and roles of the technical staff will enable the framework fully in the firm.

Key Program Roles

Table 4.8 presents the key program roles for Case Study 9.

Table 4.8   Key Program Roles for Case Study 9

Corporate Sector
Training specialist
Business Sector
Business sponsor
Business process project specialist
Governance Sector
SOA strategist
Program methodology specialist
Communications coordinator
Technology Sector
Technical sponsor
Enterprise architect
Service manager
Service domain owner

Summary of Project

Focused on the benefits of a controlled but distributed SOA, the project is an example of an evolving process improvement SOA solution.

Governance, communications, product realization, project management, architecture, service management, human resource management, and post implementation enabled the project in Case Study 9. The firm in the study is ensuring a path of a successful SOA strategy.

Key Lessons Learned on Project

- Integration of technical and business Web services into a controlled SOA contributes to continuous improvement if not competitive differential benefits for the technology department and the business departments of a firm.
- Management of enterprise services by the technology department ensures effective and economical reusability of the services.
- Training of developers in the technology department on the paradigm of service is critical for deployment and operation of SOA.

Maturity of SOA on Project

Figure 4.10 illustrates the maturity of SOA on the Case Study 9 project.

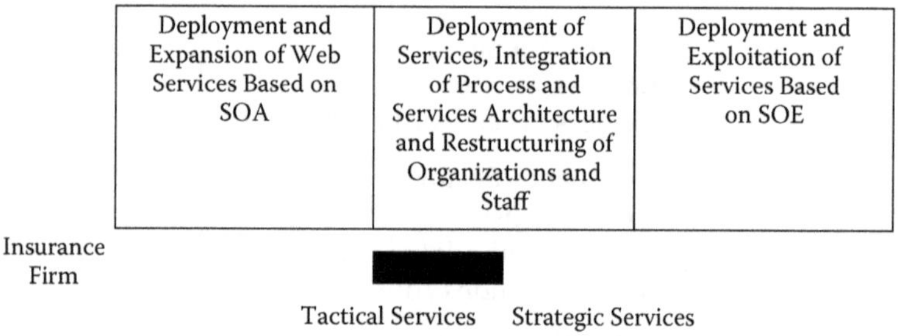

Deployment and Expansion of Web Services Based on SOA	Deployment of Services, Integration of Process and Services Architecture and Restructuring of Organizations and Staff	Deployment and Exploitation of Services Based on SOE

Insurance Firm

Tactical Services   Strategic Services

Figure 4.10   Maturity of SOA for Case Study 9 project.

Case Study 10: Municipal Energy Utility

Core Project: Internal Firm Process Integration

Background of Firm

The firm in this case study consisted of a local municipal energy utility with 350,000+ customers. Because of deregulation in the industry, the utility had to compete with nonlocal and nonmunicipal utilities. These utilities were considered better in processes of customer service than the municipal utility.

This public utility had to concurrently enhance its processes of disaster planning and recovery, and of risk management, which was evaluated at a level 2 out of 5 levels on the Capability Maturity Model Integration (CMMI), as the processes were largely informal and manual in a post-September 11 period.

The utility had to be better in business processes of risk management and customer service to compete with the other utilities.

Business Challenge

The processes of risk management and customer service were not agile enough for this municipal utility.

The bulk of the technology behind these processes were different and isolated legacy applications. The applications were designed, developed, and deployed by developers in a stovepipe technology department without effective interaction with business analysts in the business units, who were experts in customer service and in risk management. The applications were not current with Web-based methods and technologies, as the developers were experts in COBOL and were hesitant in learning new state-of-the-art technologies, which was evident in a failed pilot project to install SOA in 2004.

The utility was challenged by the technology department in that half the developers who were highly knowledgeable in the legacy applications were eligible for retirement in 2006.

The utility in this study had to deploy an *agile process* so that there would be effective enterprise risk management and improved customer service, initiated by a fully involved business staff with an SOA skilled technical staff.

Deployment of Services

The utility began the project of SOA by hiring a CIO, as a replacement to the chief technology officer (CTO) who retired in 2005. The CIO applied a new acronym to the project of not SOA but BTR (business technology realignment), which was essentially equivalent to SOA. The focus of the project was to improve the processes of customer service and risk management in an SOA.

To involve the business staff, the CIO established a defined business group of business analyst staff and current developer and architect technical staff in an effort to control the BTR project. The CIO hired a number of SOA-skilled technical staff to strengthen the group. This group effectively enabled the design, development, and deployment and governance of forthcoming risk management and customer services of SOA.

The project for the utility was enabled further because of an unanticipated disaster, as a snowstorm in 2006 caused power outages in the municipality. First, services deployed by a limited number of the new SOA skilled technical staff integrated functionality from existing applications with an ArcGlobe global positioning system (GPS) over an enterprise service bus (ESB) illustrated in Figure 4.11.

Repair and telephone service staff was empowered by component GPS services to help the 20,000+ customers impacted by the storm. The services furnished immediate identification of storm-impacted neighborhoods, so that the utility was

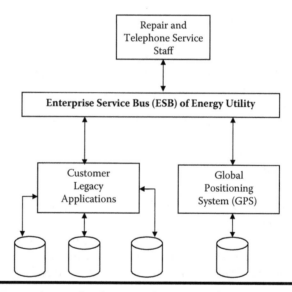

Figure 4.11 Enterprise service bus (ESB) in Case Study 10. *Note:* **The ESB allows the consumer repair and telephone service staff of the municipal energy utility to access the information in the customer applications and the GPS easily as services. This ESB forms a messaging layer for services and functions as a foundation of an SOA solution. Though ESB is a solution in this utility, services based on standards without an ESB may be an alternate strategy in other organizations.**

able to restore power sooner than in previous storms. The public image of the utility improved noticeably, due to the deployment of an initial SOA during the disaster.

An IBM WebSphere portal facilitated project deployment. This portal extracted information in the applications on power outage risk and integrated the information into an enterprise scorecard for the business units, the BTR group, and the information technology department. The scorecard furnished a foundation for the governance of services in an SOA.

This project with SOA saved the utility $50+ million in 2006, which was reinvested to improve the processes of risk management and customer service in the SOA.

Program Management Methodology: Overview

The program management methodology enabled the project with an effective and timely SOA. Figure 4.12 illustrates the methodology frameworks for Case Study 10, and Table 4.9 lists the key factors for this case study.

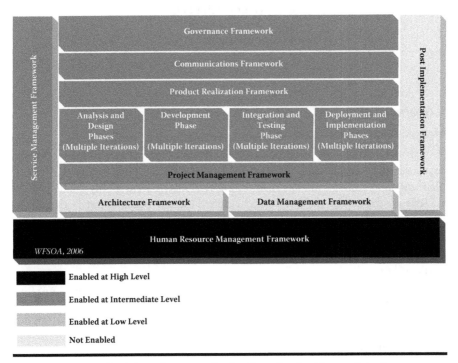

Figure 4.12   Methodology frameworks for Case Study 10: municipal energy utility.

Table 4.9   Key Factors for Case Study 10

Business Factors	Procedural Factors	Technical Factors

Financial benefits
Business client
  participation
Competitive, market,
  and regulatory
  differentials
Culture of innovation
Organizational change
  management
Executive technology
  leadership
Strategic planning
Enterprise architecture
Service orientation
Reusability of assets
	Control of program
	SOA center of competency
	Responsibilities and roles
	Education and training
	Knowledge exchange
	Change management
	Information management
	Common reference
	Naming conventions
	Technology firm
	  knowledge capture
	Risk management
	Infrastructure architecture
	Process and service
	  deployment environment
	Process and service
	  deployment techniques
	Security management
	Strategy management
		Business process
		  management product
		  software
		Middleware
		Platform of key
		  technology firms
		XML standard
		Messaging standards
		Service description
		  and discovery
		  standards
		Security standards
		Web services best
		  practices

Governance

The project was enabled by governance at an intermediate level.

Factors of control of program, financial benefits and competitive, market, and regulatory differentials from external nonlocal and nonmunicipal utilities, strategic planning, and strategy management of an initial SOA were highly evident in the BTR group formed by the CIO, who exhibited executive technology leadership, in lieu of equivalent executive business leadership. The group evaluated services and technologies important to the utility and involved business staff with technical staff. The impact of the group was enterprise architecture for the business strategy of the utility.

Governance was critical in the new SOA of the utility, but the utility was only beginning to realize the potential of SOA as a strategy.

Communications

The project was enabled by communications at an intermediate level in the deployment of the enterprise WebSphere portal scorecard, which facilitated common reference and naming conventions of technical and business terminology.

Education and training and knowledge exchange of the terminology was evident from the scorecard.

Responsibilities and roles were eventually evident with the scorecard deployed for the business units and the information technology department and for the BTR group, and security management was evident with the control of sensitive information.

Not evident was executive business leadership in proactively promoting the importance of SOA.

Product Realization

The project was enabled by product realization at an intermediate level, due to further learning of program management methodology needed by the staff.

The CIO created an SOA center of competency that included 25 analysts and developers in the technology department, of whom 20 on the pilot project in 2004 were educated in service orientation. The CIO hired an architect for the project and SOA, and had the project staff educated in business process management products, including Rational technology, and in an initial process and service deployment environment and in process and service deployment techniques, by a consulting firm. This staff was formed into five SOA analysts for capturing service requirements with service description and discovery standards (UDDI), fifteen SOA developers for developing Java routines and integrating services, and five SOA database analysts for transforming data from diverse applications into automated input.

Information management, security management, middleware, XML standard, messaging standards (SOAP), and security standards were evident in the transition.

Project Management

The project was enabled by informal project management methodology at a low level, except for change management for a culture of innovation in the utility, organizational change management, and Web services best practices, which were initiated by the CIO.

Architecture

The project was not as enabled by architecture as by product realization, communications, and governance, as infrastructure architecture was not enabled fully in the study and was at a low level.

Data Management

The project was not enabled by data management, as data management focused on disaster recovery.

Service Management

The project was enabled by service management at an intermediate level.

Process and service deployment environment was established by the CIO with consultants of the platform of the key technology firm and with business client participation of the BTR group as a service management team. This team identified a potential 70+ business processes and 15+ technical processes to convert into risk management and customer services. The processes were modeled with business process management products, which enabled identification of 50+ relevant applications, data, and technologies. The team prioritized the processes to transform into services in 2006.

Knowledge capture from the consultants of the technology firm and business process management products — if not risk management of the technology — was evident with one business analyst and one SOA analyst paired with one consultant in the modeling of a process, and reusability of assets was evident in service management by the team, but knowledge transfer to the development staff in the technology department was nonexistent.

Human Resource Management

The project was enabled by human resource management at an intermediate level, and was evident in a plan for the education and training of the technical staff and of selected business and operations staff, but completion of full training was not expected until 2008.

The CIO provided a 20 percent incentive reward to staff trained on SOA and with the utility two years beyond completion of the training.

Those who were retiring in 2005 and 2006 were rewarded by the utility if they trained replacement staff.

Post Implementation

The project was not enabled by post implementation, due to the focus of the team on customer services as an interim strategy.

Key Program Roles

Table 4.10 presents the key program roles for Case Study 10.

Table 4.10   Key Program Roles for Case Study 10

Business Sector
Business sponsor
Business process coordinator

Governance Sector
SOA strategist
Risk specialist
Technology transfer specialist
Program methodology specialist
Project planner

Technology Sector
Technical sponsor
Database analyst
SOA developer

Summary of Project

The project in Case Study 10 is a good example of a CIO effectively enabling change with disciplined governance and management of services, which positions a firm for a potentially successful SOA strategy.

Key Lessons Learned on Project

- The CIO can be *the* catalyst of change for SOA.
- Disciplined business process management and service management can be critical differentials in initiating SOA.
- Integration of business staff with skilled SOA technical staff in a governance group is critical in an SOA strategy.

Maturity of SOA on Project

Figure 4.13 illustrates the maturity of SOA for Case Study 10 project.

Deployment and Expansion of Web Services Based on SOA	Deployment of Services, Integration of Process and Services Architecture and Restructuring of Organizations and Staff	Deployment and Exploitation of Services Based on SOE

Municipal Energy Utility

Tactical Services   Strategic Services

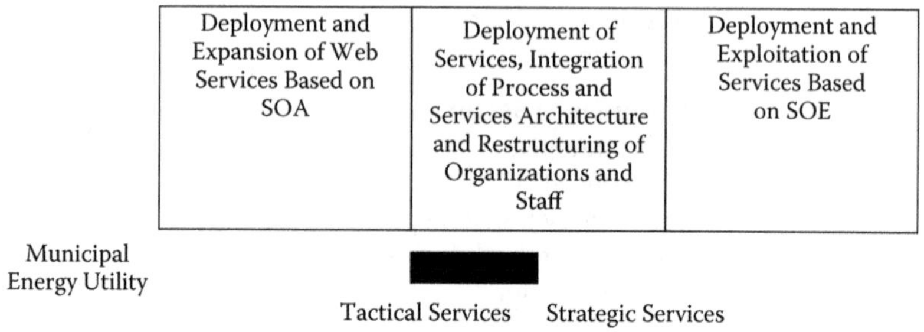

Figure 4.13   Maturity of SOA for Case Study 10 project.

Case Study 11: Banking Firm

Core Project: Internal Firm Process Integration

Background of Firm

The firm in Case Study 11 was a $3+ billion banking division of an established financial institution. The division consisted of six departments that furnished and marketed customized financial products to internal divisions of the firm and to external institutions. This division was beginning to be considered a leader in the domestic and international marketplace in new products and services. The essence of the leadership was in the low cost and the speed to the marketplace of the services. The information technology department of the firm was the enabler of the leadership.

Business Challenge

The challenge for this division was to continue as a leader in the banking industry. To be the best performer, the departments competed in the division; and developers from the technology department, who were dedicated to each of the departments, also competed in the division. Because of these conditions, the departments had applications for customized products that frequently duplicated applications and functions in the division and in the firm. Functions were manual in a few departments, but automated in other departments. Functions and applications of the departments were not effectively integrated into business processes for product development in the division. The division was essentially hindered in its goal to become a leader, if not *the* leader in the banking industry.

The division as a first mover had to deploy an *agile process* so that there would be improved time-to-market of products; an *efficient process* so that there would be less duplication and cost in the internal development of the products; and a *flexible process* so that there would be integration of functionality and teaming of staff for improved turnaround of products.

Deployment of Services

The focus of the project was to enable the division of the firm to become *the* leader in the banking industry with a solution of an SOA. To do this, the firm hired a CIO for the division who had experience in business process improvement and cultural change management in the industry. The goal of the CIO was to lead the technology department and the business departments in innovation of the product development, management, and marketing processes with integrated services.

The CIO deployed (for the technology department and the business departments) a divisional end-to-end framework for services in an SOA. This framework was designed for management processes that would service the diverse departments and the technology department through the interface of a portal. To design the framework, the CIO hired 10+ technical staff members experienced in product management processes and integrated this staff with 15+ technical and business staff members chosen by the CEO of the division for the project. For each product of the banking division, the staff identified the "what is" and the "what if" of applications and business functions, and mapped components to functions, critical data, and function and information relationships, furnishing the foundation for the framework of composite services and component services and the infrastructure of SOA. The sequence of the deployed services was determined by a few business critical success factors that could enable future leadership of the division in the banking industry.

The deployment was facilitated by a cultural change education of the technical staff and of the business staff, initiated by the CIO. Education focused on product management processes and on the reusability of services in an SOA as a divisional, not a departmental, strategy and as a business, not a technology, strategy. The initiative was enabled by the CEO evangelizing the importance of the strategy to both the division and the firm.

The deployment of the SOA was further helped by monitoring the performance of the processes and the performance and reusability of the services, as if in a utility.

The savings generated by the SOA were indicated as increased revenues of $10+ million in 2006, due to increased time-to-market of new products in weeks, not in months or years.

Program Management Methodology: Overview

The program management methodology enabled the project with an effective business unit internal solution of SOA. Figure 4.14 depicts the methodology frameworks for Case Study 11, and Table 4.11 presents the key factors for this case study.

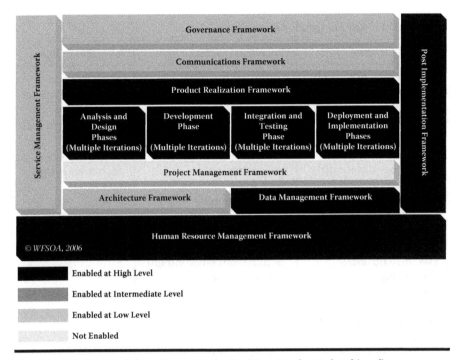

Figure 4.14   Methodology frameworks for Case Study 11: banking firm.

Table 4.11   Key Factors for Case Study 11

Business Factors	Procedural Factors	Technical Factors
Agility, efficiency, and flexibility benefits	Control of program	Internal process domain on project
Financial benefits	SOA center of competency	Internal SOA domain on project
Business client participation	Responsibilities and roles	Middleware
Competitive, market, and regulatory differentials	Education and training	Platform of key technology firms
Customer demand	Knowledge exchange	
Culture of innovation	Information management	
Organizational change management	Procurement of technology	
Executive sponsorship	Risk management	
Executive business leadership	Standards management	
Executive technology leadership	Infrastructure architecture	
Strategic planning	Process and service deployment environment	
Enterprise architecture	Process and service deployment techniques	
Focus on improvement of process	Service management and support	
Service orientation	Security management	
Reusability of assets	Continuous process improvement	
	Costing techniques	
	Strategy management	

Governance

The project was enabled by governance at an intermediate level.

Factors of agility, efficiency, and flexibility benefits; financial benefits; business client participation; competitive, market, and regulatory differentials in the industry; customer demand; organizational change management; executive sponsorship; executive business leadership; and executive technology leadership were highly evident on the project. Control of program, strategic planning to be the leader in the industry, focus on improvement of process on product development and marketing, service orientation, reusability of assets, procurement of technology, risk management, and strategy management were highly evident on the project. Product realization was highly evident as a continuous process product improvement strategy.

Although these factors enabled governance, the project was impacted by a lack of nonproprietary standards and technologies that limited governance and management to an intermediate level.

Communications

The project was enabled by communications at an intermediate level, in factors of culture of innovation, responsibilities and roles, education and training, and knowledge exchange, initiated by the CIO, and by evangelization of strategy, but a formal group managing communications was not evident on the project.

Product Realization

The project was enabled at a high level by the CIO in product realization.

Factors of process and service deployment environment, and process and service deployment techniques were highly evident on the project.

Mitigation of risk management of technologies was not evident on the project, as technologies already in the firm were included on the project, with Java and .NET as the tools of the technical staff.

This project included internal process domain and internal SOA domain.

Project Management

The project was not enabled by formal project management methodology.

Architecture

The project was enabled by architecture at an intermediate level, in factors of enterprise architecture, infrastructure architecture, and security management of the firm, middleware and platform of key technology firms, and in integration of product management staff on an interim architecture team, but was enabled by non-open proprietary technologies, which limit a first-mover strategy.

Data Management

The project was enabled by data management at a high level, which was extensive in data mapping and data modeling, and meticulous in information management.

Service Management

The project was enabled by service management at an intermediate level, in meta-data service management and support, in costing techniques in SLAs, and in standards management, but the business staff deferred to the technical staff.

Human Resource Management

The project was enabled by human resource management at a high level, in the education and training of technical staff and business staff on product management processes and strategy management.

Post Implementation

The project was enabled by post implementation at a high level, in continued education and training of the staff through an implemented SOA center of competency and an internal university.

Key Program Roles

Table 4.12 presents the key program roles for Case Study 11.

Table 4.12   Key Program Roles for Case Study 11

Corporate Sector Executive sponsor
Business Sector Business sponsor
Governance Sector SOA strategist Asset librarian Communications coordinator Technology transfer specialist
Technology Sector Technical sponsor Service availability administrator Infrastructure architect

Summary of Project

The project in Case Study 11 is an example of an SOA deployment for a division of a firm, which is enabling the division to enhance its product leadership in an industry. The project in the study may be a prototype of an enterprise SOA to be deployed in the firm.

Key Lessons Learned on Project

- The CIO can be an agent of change for business process improvement in a firm.
- Communication between business staff and technical staff is critical on a project of SOA.
- Focus on improvement of process in an SOA is critical for product leadership in an industry.
- Integration of new product management methodology staff with technology staff is helpful on a project of SOA.
- SOA may be instrumental in a first-mover strategy.

Maturity of SOA on Project

Figure 4.15 illustrates the maturity of SOA on the Case Study 11 project.

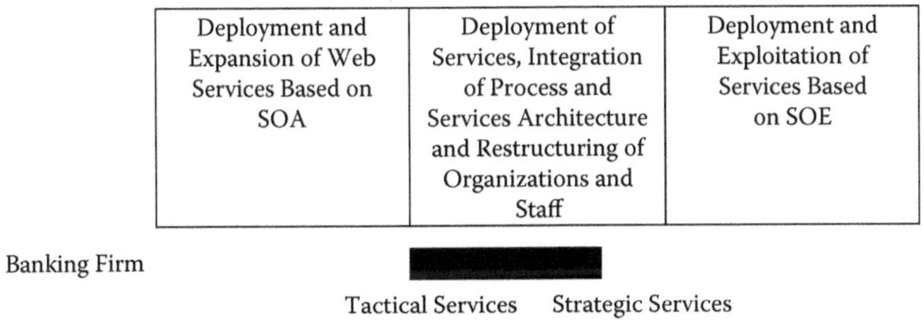

Deployment and Expansion of Web Services Based on SOA	Deployment of Services, Integration of Process and Services Architecture and Restructuring of Organizations and Staff	Deployment and Exploitation of Services Based on SOE

Banking Firm

Tactical Services   Strategic Services

Figure 4.15   Maturity of SOA for Case Study 11 project.

Case Study 12: Telecommunications Firm

Core Project: Internal Firm Process Integration

Background of Firm

The firm in Case Study 12 was a large telecommunications business created from acquisitions of smaller firms in its industry. This firm generated a daily 3+ million customer transactions in 2000+ stores in 2005, based on deployed Web services by the information technology departments in the business units of the smaller firms. This firm had the largest deployment of services in our studies, due to the smaller firms.

Business Challenge

The challenge for the firm was that the deployment of the services was not contributing to a competitively agile, efficient, or flexible business.

Services were deployed inconsistently in the business units of the full firm and were duplicated an estimated 15 to 30 times in the units. Services were named inconsistently by the developers in the technology departments and by the business analysts in the business units. Standards were nonexistent in the technology departments and the units. Reusability of services was not feasible in the firm. Ownership of the services was not formalized in the firm.

Because of these conditions, the firm could not adapt to customer opportunities as an enterprise as fast as competitor firms in the telecommunications industry.

The firm in this study had to clearly deploy an *efficient operation* so that there would be less cost and duplication of services, an *agile process* so that there would be enterprise ownership standards for faster integration of core services, and a *flexible process* so that there would be immediate reusability of services.

Deployment of an enterprise SOA was critical for the firm.

Deployment of Services

The focus of the project was to evolve from uncontrolled Web services to an effective enterprise SOA solution. To do this, the smaller technology departments merged into a larger-sized technology department for the firm. The new department invested in a customized but proprietary service management "workbench," which furnished a Web-based portal with best practices guidelines for deployment of composite and component services in an SOA and is illustrated in Figure 4.16.

The portal included an infrastructure layer that published a UDDI registry of services and subscribers in the business units of the full firm. Finally, the workbench furnished access to best-of-class software for the developer staff in the technology department and to project management software for the business staff in the business units.

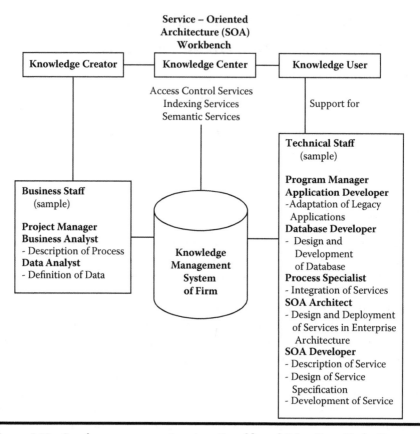

Figure 4.16   Service management system "workbench" for Case Study 12.

The workbench also furnished orchestration software that facilitated externalized integration of legacy applications of the internal smaller firms into 45+ composite services of the merged firm. CICS transactions with external partnered firms were exposed as component services with SOA Software technology, and the security of the transactions was furnished with SOA Software Partner Gateway technology. Service level agreements (SLAs) were introduced with the internal business units of the merged firm and with external partnered firms.

Upon deployment of the SOA in 2006, the firm decreased the budget for technology by 50 percent in elimination of duplicate services and in having 40 percent in reusability of services.

Program Management Methodology: Overview

The program management methodology effectively enabled the project with an effective enterprise SOA solution. Figure 4.17 illustrates the methodology frameworks for Case Study 12, and Table 4.13 presents the key factors for this case study.

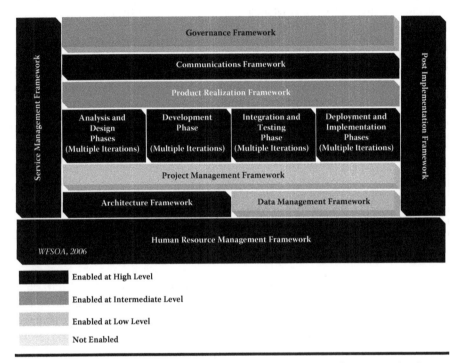

Figure 4.17   Methodology frameworks for Case Study 12: telecommunications firm.

Table 4.13　Key Factors for Case Study 12

Business Factors	Procedural Factors	Technical Factors
Agility, efficiency, and flexibility benefits Financial benefits Business client participation Organizational change management Executive technology leadership Strategic planning Service orientation Reusability of assets	Control of program Responsibilities and roles Education and training Knowledge exchange Change management Information management Common reference Naming conventions Procurement of technology Standards management Infrastructure architecture Process and service deployment environment Process and service deployment techniques Service catalog management Service management and support Security management Costing techniques	External SOA domain on project Business process management product software Middleware Platform of key technology firms Platform specialty tools from platform technology firm Proprietary technologies Best-of-class tools XML standard Messaging standards Service description and discovery standards Web services best practices

Governance

The project was enabled by governance at an intermediate level.

Factors of control of program; in having service orientation in an SOA; agility, efficiency, and flexibility benefits; financial benefits; organizational change management; and strategic planning were highly evident on the project. Process and service deployment techniques with standards management were evident in the deployment of the proprietary service management technology workbench. Procurement of technology was evident in the integration of nonproprietary and proprietary software technologies.

Further evidence of executive business leadership was not tangible in governance; also, executive sponsorship was not tangible on the project.

Communications

The project was enabled by communications at a high level in the deployment of the workbench.

The foundation of the project was the workbench, which furnished a forum for knowledge exchange and interaction of technical and business staff on the project. Common reference, naming conventions, standards management, rigorous service catalog management, security management, and Web services best practices were evident with the workbench. Responsibilities and roles and knowledge exchange of the staff were facilitated with the workbench.

The workbench was *the* enabler of the SOA in this study.

Product Realization

The project was enabled by product realization at an intermediate level.

Factors of process and service deployment techniques were evident in service development for component granular services, service composition for integration of services, service testing for functional requirements and security of services, and service performance and publishing on the project. Techniques facilitated the process and service deployment environment of the SOA, so that consumers of services in the business units could search contract metadata in the firm on the workbench, in an effort to discover requested services. Business process management products were helpful but were limited in process and service deployment techniques.

This project included external SOA domain.

Project Management

The project was enabled by formal project management at a low level, except for executive technology leadership of the CIO of the merged firm, who focused on reusability of assets as the business and technical strategy of the SOA.

Architecture

The project was enabled by architecture at a high level.

The SOA infrastructure architecture factor was evident in the layers of user interface, business, core and interface services, and technical services, which were integrated in ESB middleware, and factor of best-in-class tools was evident in the procurement of SOA Software technology as a platform and specialty tool and in the proprietary technology workbench.

XML standard and messaging standards were evident on the project.

Data Management

The project was enabled by data management at a low level in information management, in the initiation of transforming data in the legacy applications of the acquired smaller firms to services.

Service Management

The project was enabled by service management at a high level, in the factors of business client participation and change management, which facilitated identification of existing core processes to be converted to services and inclusion of future critical processes to be migrated to services.

The project was helped by service description and discovery standards as well as Web services best practices.

Human Resource Management

The project was fully enabled by human resource management at a high level, in the service orientation training of the developer technical staff of the small firms. Training included the workbench.

Post Implementation

The project was enabled by post implementation at a high level, in service management and support with the new workbench. In the merged firm, the workbench furnished costing techniques for the operations of services, dashboards for monitoring the performance of services in the SOA, and facilities for improving the performance of the services.

This workbench was instrumental in less redundancy of rogue services throughout the business units of the merged firm.

Key Program Roles

Table 4.14 presents the key program roles for Case Study 12.

Table 4.14   Key Program Roles for Case Study 12

Corporate Sector Training specialist
Governance Sector SOA strategist SOA program coordinator Service librarian Communications coordinator Program methodology specialist
Technology Sector Technical sponsor Infrastructure architect Service manager SOA developer

Summary of Project

The project in Case Study 12 is a very good example of a controlled and effective deployment of an SOA solution, following a chaotic and noncontrolled deployment of Web services.

Key Lessons Learned on Project

- Central governance of services can contribute to an effective SOA solution.
- Cooperation of enterprise technology staff and business staff in the design, development, and management of services can contribute to and is required for good governance of SOA.
- Enterprise focus of staff can contribute to faster identification of core processes to convert to services in an SOA.
- Internal innovation in portal and service software technologies and tools can contribute to helpful integration of services in an SOA.
- Service orientation training of technology staff remains critical in solutions and strategy of SOA.

Maturity of SOA on Project

Figure 4.18 illustrates the maturity of SOA for Case Study 12 project.

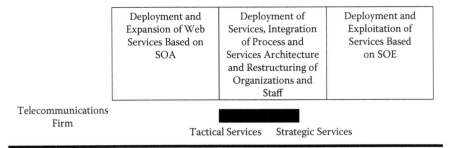

Deployment and Expansion of Web Services Based on SOA	Deployment of Services, Integration of Process and Services Architecture and Restructuring of Organizations and Staff	Deployment and Exploitation of Services Based on SOE

Telecommunications Firm

Tactical Services   Strategic Services

Figure 4.18   Maturity of SOA for Case Study 12 project.

Case Study 13: Software Firm

Core Project: Internal Firm Process Integration

Background of Firm

The firm in Case Study 13 was a growing international software business marketing simple Web services technology. This firm was generating less in revenue in contrast to large technology firms in the industry. The personnel in the firm were mostly technical staff not educated in the business intricacies of current and future customers or in the business applications of complex SOA.

Business Challenge

The challenge for the firm was to change the business so as to become considered both customer and SOA knowledgeable. The staff in the information technology department of the firm generally engaged fellow technical staff in the technology departments of customers, not business staff, and evaluated Web services software as technology, not business support. Information on the businesses of the customers was not enough for the technical staff to become knowledgeable on internal processes, and information on their industries was not enough for the staff to become knowledgeable of trends. Information on SOA was not enough for them to become knowledgeable of technological trends. Although the firm had excellent Web services software, the technology was not marketed by a savvy marketing department, but rather by the staff of the technology department.

The firm in this study had to deploy an *agile process* for its technical staff to become educated in the business fundamentals of the customers, so that the business, customer, and technical expertise of the staff and of the firm would be equivalent to larger technology firms. The firm had to demonstrate business and technical expertise, in an effort to be engaged with products of intermediate to complex SOA. Finally, the firm had to market the expertise, so that it would be able to partner with larger software technology firms on solutions of SOA, and have a process to manage learning of the technical staff.

Deployment of Services

The focus of the project was to enhance the customer and business knowledge of the technology department of the firm through an internal SOA solution. SOA furnished composite services to a current client/server CRM application and an ERP application, both of which had engagement information on existing customers. Information in the applications was improved to include input of best practices and worst practices of the department with future customers. SOA further integrated component services for Web-based education of the staff from external portals of business schools. This solution of SOA was instrumental in an increase of projects and an increase in $40+ million revenues in 2006.

Software on the project was essentially Microsoft technology.

Program Management Methodology: Overview

The program management methodology enabled the project with an effective but limited solution of SOA. Figure 4.19 illustrates the methodology frameworks for Case Study 13, and Table 4.15 presents the key factors for this case study.

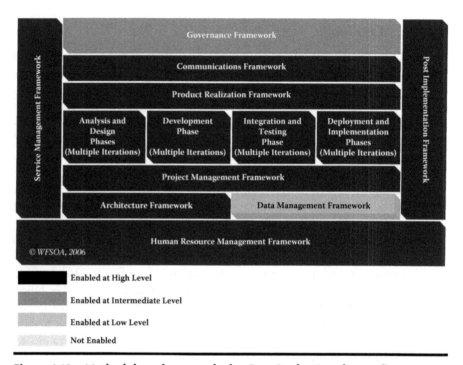

Figure 4.19 Methodology frameworks for Case Study 13: software firm.

Table 4.15   Key Factors for Case Study 13

Business Factors	Procedural Factors	Technical Factors
Agility, efficiency, and flexibility benefits	Control of program	Internal SOA domain on project
Financial benefits	Responsibilities and roles	External SOA domain on project
Business client participation	Education and training	Business process management product software
Customer demand	Knowledge exchange	Middleware
Culture of innovation	Change management	Platform of key technology firms
Executive sponsorship	Information management	Platform specialty tools from platform technology firm
Executive business leadership	Common reference	XML standard
Executive technology leadership	Naming conventions	Messaging standards
Focus on improvement of process	Procurement of technology	Security standards
Service orientation	Risk management	User interface standards
	Standards management	Web services best practices
	Infrastructure architecture	
	Process and service deployment environment	
	Process and service deployment techniques	
	Service management and support	
	Security management	
	Continuous process improvement	
	Costing techniques	

Governance

The project was enabled by informal governance at an intermediate level and was evident in business client participation, executive business leadership, executive technology leadership, and executive sponsorship, which focused on control of program, service orientation, and Web services best practices. Common reference and naming conventions of CRM and ERP terminology were evident on the project. Culture of innovation in the information technology department of the firm was helpful on the project.

Focus on improvement of process was a goal.

Improved focusing on strategic planning was not evident initially on the project.

Communications

The project was enabled by communications at a high level and was noticeably evident in knowledge exchange from the technology firm to the internal staff and from the internal staff to the customer organization staff.

User interface standards with ERP and CRM were also evident on the project.

Project Realization

The project was enabled by product realization at a high level, in factor of process and service deployment environment from the platform and specialty tools of Microsoft, which facilitated flexibility, efficiency, and agility benefits and financial benefits from customer engagements.

This project included internal SOA domain and external SOA domain.

Project Management

The project was enabled by project management at a high level, in procurement of BizTalk business process management product software of Microsoft, in simple infrastructure architecture; and in responsibilities and roles and education and training of selected staff on the technology.

Architecture

The project was enabled by architecture at a high level, in middleware, XML standard, messaging standards, and security standards on the new services, due to expertise in diverse infrastructure architecture for customer engagements.

Data Management

The project was enabled by information management, risk management, and standards management at a low level, due to linking to nonofficial data standards.

Service Management

The project was enabled by customer demand for expertise in the businesses of the customers and by change management and security management of the services consistent with conditions and trends in industry and standards management at a high level.

Costing techniques were helpful on the project.

Process and service deployment techniques were also helpful on the project.

Human Resource Management

The project was enabled by education and training and knowledge exchange of selected technical staff at a high level.

Post Implementation

The project was enabled by service management and support at a high level, in the monitoring of the services, which ensured continuous process improvement in the firm.

Key Program Roles

Table 4.16 presents the key program roles for Case Study 13.

Table 4.16 Key Program Roles for Case Study 13

Corporate Sector	Governance Sector
Training specialist	SOA program coordinator
	Knowledge coordinator
Business Sector	Asset librarian
Business analyst for	
extended organization	**Technology Sector**
Business process coordinator	Infrastructure architect
Business process project	Integration specialist
specialist	Security administrator

Summary of Project

The project in Case Study 13 is an example of a growing firm, which in deployment of services gained continuous improvement of a neglected process, and which may deploy further solutions in an SOA strategy.

Key Lessons Learned on Project

- Choice of a *bona fide* SOA technology firm can contribute to fast deployment of services.
- Incremental deployment of SOA can help growing firms in an industry.

Maturity of SOA on Project

Figure 4.20 illustrates the maturity of SOA on Case Study 13 project.

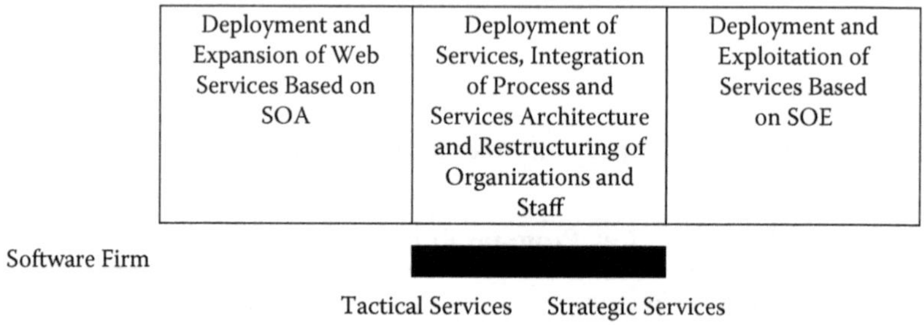

Deployment and Expansion of Web Services Based on SOA	Deployment of Services, Integration of Process and Services Architecture and Restructuring of Organizations and Staff	Deployment and Exploitation of Services Based on SOE

Software Firm

Tactical Services   Strategic Services

Figure 4.20   Maturity of SOA for Case Study 13 project.

Chapter 5 discusses deployment and exploitation of services based on SOE.

Chapter 5

Deployment and Exploitation of Services Based on SOE

This chapter discusses the deployment and exploitation of services based on SOE in an automobile research firm (Case Study 14) and a health care consortium (Case Study 15).

Case Study 14: Automobile Research Firm

Core Project: External Firm Process Integration

Background of Firm

This study involved a medium-sized automobile research firm. The function of the firm was to compile registration and sales information from the data of 250+ automotive, financial, governmental, insurance, and marketing agencies and firms in the United States and Canada. Information was estimated to be 1.5 petabytes (quadrillions) on 500+ million automobiles and 250+ million households from 3+ billion transactions annually. Growth of the information was estimated to be 30 percent annually. This firm customized and furnished the information as a data mining product in monthly national sales reports to dealers and manufacturers in the industry that depended on the reports for inventory strategy.

The concern of executive management of the firm was in the availability of the monthly reports. The reports were available for offline distribution to manufacturers and dealers 30 days after the end of a month, because compilation of the information required 30 days. Although the data for the information was in the databases of the firm following file input from the firms and agencies in the industry, the customization of the data into information and the distribution of the reports were offline processes. Dealers and manufacturers were not able to effectively market automobiles in locales based on the intelligence in the reports, due to the lateness of the reports. They demanded the reports within ten days following month end.

The internal processes of generating the monthly reports were based on antiquated legacy applications.

Business Challenge

These processes were not agile, efficient, or flexible for the firm, as the legacy applications were developed beginning in 1976. Changes in the databases of the firm, due to governmental information privacy regulations and industry requirements, and in the reports, due to manufacturer requests, were cumbersome to do in the applications. Data was normally processed in jobs with as many as 50+ steps. Errors in the data resulted in a repeat of the steps. Manual errors in resolving original errors resulted in a repetition of the steps. The firm was not able to compete for the businesses of current and future dealers and manufacturers that continued to demand improvements.

The automobile research firm had to deploy *agile processes* so that there would be faster adaptation to customer demand, *efficient processes* so that there would be faster compilation, customization and distribution of information and reports, and *flexible processes* so that there would be faster improvement to the applications of the business.

Deployment of services as a solution had to contribute to a competitive equivalency strategy, if not a continuous improvement strategy.

Deployment of Services

The focus of this project was to have flexible, efficient, and agile operations and improved processes of reporting. Cost reduction was a further focus of the project. The solution was automation of an SOA, based on existing legacy applications, consistent with service standards, and designed, developed, integrated, and deployed in a subsidiary of the automobile research firm.

SOA enabled a foundation for the improved processes. Business compilation, customization, and distribution rules were extracted from the legacy applications for services. Data capture, data conversion in XML from automobile identification codes, data enhancement, data extraction, data standardization, database creation, master database management, performance management, reference management, and service management were provided as component services. Services were integrated into composite services in less than three months. The composition of the services auto-mated the compilation, customization, and distribution of information and reports and included Informatica, Oracle, Red Hat, SAS, and Tibco technologies.

SOA enabled data file input from the marketing, insurance, governmental, financial, and automotive firms and agencies to be compiled immediately in min-utes not hours and in one step not 50+ steps. Customization improved by 50 per-cent in online processing. The cost of online operations was 7 percent lower than offline processing, due to faster error detection, improved quality control, and fewer operations staff in the subsidiary. Reports were available for online distribution to manufacturers and dealers on the Web ten days following customization or ten days following the end of the month. SOA produced a tangible solution.

Program Management Methodology: Overview

The program management methodology enabled the project of this study with an effective business unit solution of SOA with diverse technology firms. Figure 5.1 illustrates the methodology frameworks for Case Study 14, and Table 5.1 provides the key factors in this case study.

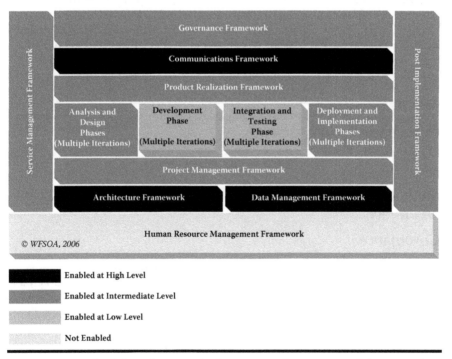

Figure 5.1 Methodology frameworks for Case Study 14: automobile research firm.

Table 5.1   Key Factors for Case Study 14

Business Factors	Procedural Factors	Technical Factors
Agility, efficiency, and flexibility benefits	Control of program	Internal SOA domain on project
Financial benefits	Change management	External SOA domain on project
Business client participation	Information management	Business process management product software
Competitive, market, and regulatory differentials	Common reference	Data tools
Customer demand	Naming conventions	Middleware
Culture of innovation	Procurement of technology	Platform of key technology firms
Executive sponsorship	Risk management	Platform specialty tools from platform technology firm
Executive technology leadership	Standards management	Proprietary technologies
Strategic planning	Infrastructure architecture	Best-of-class tools
Focus on improvement of process	Process and service deployment environment	XML standard
Service orientation	Process and service deployment techniques	Messaging standards
Reusability of assets	Service catalog management	Service description and discovery standards
	Service management and support	Security standards
	Security management	User interface standards
	Continuous process improvement	
	Strategy management	

Note: Definitions of *factors* are in Table 2.2 in Chapter 2 and may be referenced in more than one framework.

Methodology Frameworks and Key Factor Highlights on Project

Governance

The project was enabled by governance at an intermediate level.

Factors of agility, efficiency, and flexibility benefits; competitive, market, and regulatory differentials; customer demand; focus on improvement of process; business control of program; strategic planning; service orientation; and reusability of assets were defined by business client participation of the business unit, with the help of a consulting firm, and were highly evident on the project.

Factors of risk management, standards management, service catalog management, service description and discovery standards, XML standard, and user interface standards were evident on the project, with the help of the firm's information technology department.

Not evident was executive technology leadership or executive business leadership in the framework of governance, although executive sponsorship with consulting firm help was evident on the project.

Communications

The project was enabled by communications at a high level.

Consensus on justification of the SOA contributed to the creation of the SOA.

Further communications on the criticality of common reference and naming conventions were highly evident as factors ensuring information management in the SOA.

Product Realization

The project was enabled by generally informal product realization at an intermediate to low level, due to low integration of the development and integration and testing phases.

Procurement of technology, process and service deployment environment, and process and service deployment techniques were evident as factors in the design and deployment of interfaces for dealers and manufacturers.

Business process management product software, data tools, and best-of-class tools were evident on the project.

This project included internal SOA domain and external SOA domain.

Project Management

The project was enabled by informal project management at an intermediate level.

Executive technology leadership of the technology department with interim consulting staff was evident on initial services, and financial benefits from investment in SOA were evident as a factor in time-to-market of the SOA.

Culture of innovation was helpful on the project.

Architecture

The project was enabled by architecture at a high level.

Service orientation was highly evident and instrumental in integrating security management, messaging standards, and security standards in the SOA.

Platform of key technology firms and platform specialty tools from platform technology firms were helpful, and middleware and proprietary technologies were included on this project.

Data Management

The project was enabled by data management at a high level in information management and infrastructure architecture that facilitated file processing of XML and quality.

Service Management

The project was enabled by service management at an intermediate level, due to a focus on information requirements that was minimal.

Change management in continuous process improvement was highly evident, however with service management and support and strategy management, in focusing on core functionality to be configured as services in the SOA strategy.

Human Resource Management

The project was not as enabled by human resource management as by the other frameworks, although the project was designed by dedicated business unit staff, developed and integrated by contracted consulting staff, and deployed by dedicated technology department staff.

Education and training of the technology staff on SOA was essentially not evident on the project. Responsibilities and roles of the technology staff and of the business staff were not evident on the initial project.

Post Implementation

The project was enabled by post implementation at an intermediate level, due to a lack of service level agreements (SLAs).

Key Program Roles

Table 5.2 provides the key program roles for Case Study 14.

Table 5.2   Key Program Roles for Case Study 14

Business Sector	Technology Sector
Business sponsor	Technical sponsor
Governance Sector	Database analyst
SOA strategist	Database administrator
Process specialist	Infrastructure architect
Procurement specialist	Security specialist

Summary of Project

The project in Case Study 14 is an excellent example of a business unit SOA solution in a medium-sized firm. Dedicated business staff planned a competitive equivalency strategy. The project in the study resulted in a continuous and scalable improvement strategy.

Key Lessons Learned on Project

- Choice of off-the-shelf technology can accelerate delivery and deployment of services solutions.
- Dedicated emphasis on improving a non-agile, inefficient, and inflexible process, and in a defined subsidiary of a firm, can contribute to deployment of services that satisfy consumer firms.
- Focus on service orientation training of internal technical staff from the beginning of a project could expand the potential of an SOA strategy.

Maturity of SOA on Project

Figure 5.2 illustrates the maturity of SOA for Case Study 14.

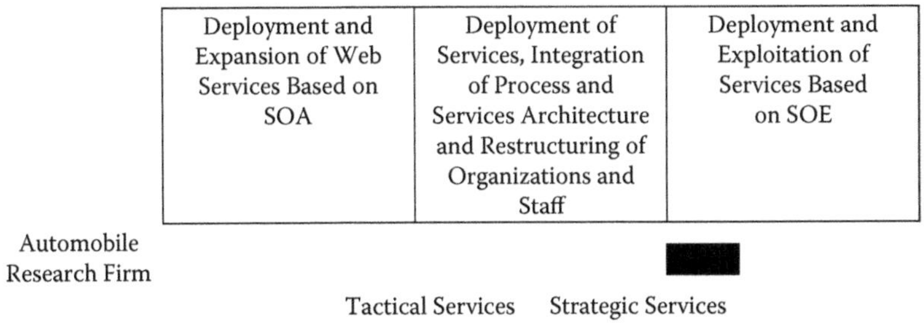

Deployment and Expansion of Web Services Based on SOA	Deployment of Services, Integration of Process and Services Architecture and Restructuring of Organizations and Staff	Deployment and Exploitation of Services Based on SOE

Automobile Research Firm

　　　　　　　　　　Tactical Services　　　Strategic Services

Figure 5.2　Maturity of SOA on Case Study 14 project.

Case Study 15: Health Care Consortium

Core Project: External Firm Process Integration

Background of Consortium

This final case study involved a health-care consortium of insurers, hospitals, and doctors that had an annual $9+ billion in revenue in 2004. The function of the consortium was to process a monthly 10+ million invoices, payments, and reimbursements of members. The processing was done electronically and manually in inconsistent codes, data definitions, and entry and file formats, between legacy applications of doctor, hospital and insurer participants, and of state and federal agencies.

Business Challenge

The process was costly and inefficient for the consortium, as costs were the highest in the country, and inflexible with legislated American National Standards Institute (ANSI) Health Insurance Portability and Accountability Act (HIPAA) format standards of the federal government. Due to legislation, the consortium had to conform to consistent ANSI X12N837 format and coding standards in the description and in the exchange of patient information between insurer, hospital, and doctor applications.

The consortium had to deploy an *efficient process* so that there would be compliance with HIPAA and consistency in the exchange of patient information. The process had to be less costly than current operations. The consortium had to concurrently deploy a *flexible process* so that there would be fast integration of patient information from current and future doctor, hospital, and insurer applications, but with the information in continual control by the participants.

The consortium was confronted with considerations for deployment of an improved process, including:

- Create a centralized application that could be accessed by the insurer, hospital, and doctor participants and discontinue the applications of the participants; or
- Create a common database containing patient information that could be accessed by each of the applications; or
- Deploy a common gateway middleware SOA that could offer information for services to interoperate on a network, without having to change the applications of the participants, and that could be accessed by each of the applications

Only one of these considerations was feasible for the information technology department of the consortium, and that was the common gateway middleware SOA solution.

Deployment of Services

The consortium decided that the primary focus of the project should be an SOA for processing patient information between the doctor, hospital, and insurer applications that conformed to HIPAA standards, but a secondary focus in having an SOA was to cut the cost of the operations.

The information technologists of the consortium and of the participants as an ad hoc team deployed Web services in servers at participant insurer, hospital, and doctor offices. Software formatted information to HIPAA standards, furnished the information as component and composite services, and transmitted the information on a proprietary and secure virtual private network (VPN) between consortium participants. The gateway SOA was a flexible solution that enabled the participants to be in continued control of patient information already customized in their local applications.

The SOA that integrated HIPAA standards saved an annual $10+ million in consortium and participant operations in 2005 and an estimated $40+ million and further savings of 80 percent in processing time in 2006. The SOA was such an organizational success story that other health-care organizations were studying the strategy in this study. The SOA used Microsoft technologies.

Program Management Methodology: Overview

The program management methodology enabled the project with an effective and immediate solution of SOA with existing legacy applications of diverse participants.

Figure 5.3 illustrates the methodology frameworks for Case Study 15, and Table 5.3 provides the key factors for this case study.

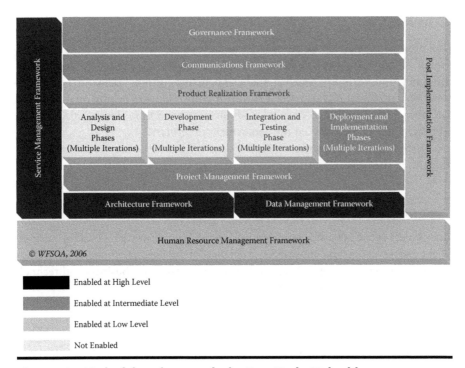

Enabled at High Level

Enabled at Intermediate Level

Enabled at Low Level

Not Enabled

Figure 5.3   Methodology frameworks for Case Study 15: health care consortium.

Table 5.3   Key Factors for Case Study 15

Business Factors	Procedural Factors	Technical Factors
Agility, efficiency, and flexibility benefits	Control of program Responsibilities and roles Knowledge exchange	External process domain on project External SOA domain on
Financial benefits	Change management	project
Business client participation	Information management Common reference	Data tools Middleware
Customer demand	Naming conventions	Platform of key
Culture of innovation	Risk management Infrastructure architecture	technology firms Platform specialty tools
Executive technology leadership	Process and service deployment techniques Security management	from platform technology firm Proprietary technologies
Strategic planning Service orientation Reusability of assets	Continuous process improvement Costing techniques	XML standard Messaging standards

Governance

The project was enabled by governance at an intermediate level, in factors of control of program and continuous process improvement; costing techniques; agility, efficiency, and flexibility benefits; financial benefits; customer demand; service orientation; and reusability of assets. Culture of innovation was helpful on the project. Members of the insurance, hospital, and doctor organizations formed a committee of governance that controlled the deployment of services.

Further executive business leadership in the framework of governance was not evident on the project.

Communications

The project was enabled by communications at an intermediate level, in business client participation and knowledge exchange of intellectual property as well as service solutions by the participants, but not with executive business and technology leadership in proactively promoting SOA.

Product Realization

The project was enabled by product realization in process and service deployment techniques in a formal deployment phase, but at a generally low level was not enabled in analysis and design, development and integration, and testing phases.

This project included external process domain and external SOA domain.

Project Management

The project was enabled by project management at an intermediate level, in the executive technology leadership of the CIO of the central consortium and the inclusion of information technologists from the organizations that were on a steering committee. This committee managed strategic planning, change management, and risk management.

The project, however, was managed by a consulting firm, which implemented the infrastructure architecture with the business staff and the technical team.

Architecture

The project was enabled by architecture at a high level, in security management, XML standard, and messaging standards (SOAP), which functioned in high performance, scalability, and security.

Platform specialty tools from the platform technology firm and proprietary technologies were included in the project.

Data Management

The project was enabled by data management at a high level, in information management, common reference, naming conventions, data tools for data translation, and data matching middleware, with HIPAA ANSI standards.

Service Management

The project was enabled by service management at a high level, with the help of the consulting firm in initiating participant patient information services on the project.

Human Resource Management

The project was enabled by human resource management at a low level, due to lack of an organizational change management program.

Post Implementation

The project was enabled by post implementation at a low level, due to lack of service management reporting and reviews.

Key Project Roles

Table 5.4 provides the key project roles for Case Study 15.

Table 5.4   Key Project Roles for Case Study 15

Business Sector	Technology Sector
Business client	Technical sponsor
Business process project specialist	Database analyst
	Security specialist
Governance Sector	Infrastructure architect
SOA program coordinator	Deployment specialist
Knowledge coordinator	

Summary of Project

The project in Case Study 15 is an example of fast compliance with demands of governmental regulation in a simple but timely solution of SOA and of strategy.

Key Lessons Learned on Project

- Collaboration of diverse business entities and technical staff in a crisis can contribute to fast deployment of an SOA solution.
- Legacy applications can be intelligently integrated in an SOA solution.
- Savings in costs of processes may be an unexpected benefit from an initial SOA solution.

Maturity of SOA on Project

Figure 5.4 illustrates the maturity of SOA for Case Study 15.

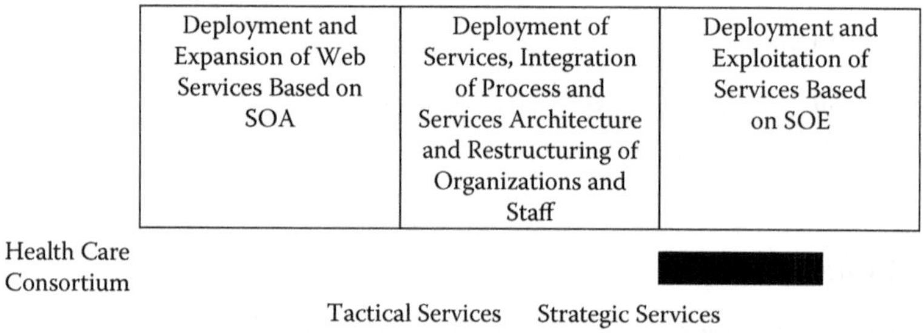

Deployment and Expansion of Web Services Based on SOA	Deployment of Services, Integration of Process and Services Architecture and Restructuring of Organizations and Staff	Deployment and Exploitation of Services Based on SOE

Health Care Consortium

Tactical Services   Strategic Services

Figure 5.4   Maturity of SOA on Case Study 15 project.

We conclude our findings from deployment and expansion of Web services based on SOA, deployment of services, integration of process and services architecture and restructuring of organizations and staff, and deployment and exploitation of services based on SOE in Chapter 6.

Chapter 6

Conclusion

The program management methodology of this book is demonstrated in the frameworks of the methodology, in the key factors for enabling the frameworks, in the key roles of program staff, in the key lessons learned on the projects, and in the maturity of SOA in our studies.

Frameworks of Methodology for SOA

The frameworks of the methodology for SOA demonstrated enablement for governance, communications, product realization, project management, architecture, data management, service management, human resource management, and post implementation on the projects in our studies. The projects are enabled at a high level of methodology (29.6 percent*), at an intermediate level (34.8 percent*), at a low level (20 percent*), and not at all (15.6 percent*). Table 6.1 displays the findings on the frameworks.

Architecture, service management, post implementation, data management, and product realization are cited as enabled more frequently at a high level than governance, human resource management, communications, and project management on the projects in the studies. Encouraging is the higher frequency of enablement at high (29.6 percent) or intermediate (34.8 percent) levels than at low (20 percent) or not at all (15.6 percent) levels, as most of the business firms continue to evolve on their projects to deployment and exploitation of services based on SOE, as further displayed in in Figure 6.1. Findings are clear that business firms in our recent studies continue to evolve in the methodology of SOA strategy.

---

* Citation frequency percentage of framework enablement = Number of citations/(9 Frameworks × 15 Firms in studies).

Table 6.1   Frameworks of Methodology for SOA

Frameworks of Methodology	High Citation	Intermediate Citation	Low Citation	Not at All Citation
Governance	4	8	3	0
Communications	3	7	3	2
Product realization	5	5	4	1
Project management	1	4	4	6
Architecture	7	7	1	0
Data management	5	1	6	3
Service management	6	6	1	2
Human resource management	4	4	3	4
Post implementation	5	5	2	3
	40	47	27	21
	29.6%	**34.8%**	**20%**	**15.6%**

Key Factors for Enabling Frameworks of Methodology

Key business factors (70.7 percent*) are more enabling than key technical factors (55.3 percent*) in the frameworks of the methodology on the projects of our studies of SOA. Procedural factors (68.4 percent*) are also more enabling than technical factors. Findings continue to confirm the results of our study of Web services in 2004, in which business factors were found to be more important than technical factors of services in firms.

Key factor findings are displayed in Tables 6.2, 6.3, and 6.4.

---

* Citation frequency percentage of business, procedural, and technical factors = Number of business, procedural, or technical author citations/(15 Business, 22 Procedural, or 20 Technical factors × 15 Firms).

Business Factors

Table 6.2   Key Business Factors for Enabling Frameworks of Methodology

Business Factors	Citation Frequency
Agility, efficiency, and flexibility benefits	14
Financial benefits	13
Business client participation	11
Competitive, market, and regulatory differentials	11
Customer demand	11
Culture of innovation	11
Organizational change management	8
Executive sponsorship	6
Executive business leadership	4
Executive technology leadership	13
Strategic planning	12
Enterprise architecture	4
Focus on improvement of process	12
Service orientation	15
Reusability of assets	14
	70.7%

Service orientation; agility, efficiency, and flexibility benefits; reusability of assets; financial benefits; and executive technology leadership are cited frequently on the projects in the studies, as shown in Table 6.2. Strategic planning and focus on improvement of process are cited as drivers on the projects. Business client participation; competitive, market, and regulatory differentials; customer demand; and culture of innovation are cited frequently as enablers of the projects.

Procedural Factors

Table 6.3 presents the key procedural factors for enabling the frameworks of methodology on the projects.

Table 6.3 Key Procedural Factors for Enabling Frameworks of Methodology

Procedural Factors	*Citation Frequency*
Control of program	14
SOA center of competency	6
Responsibilities and roles	12
Education and training	8
Knowledge exchange	11
Change management	12
Information management	12
Common reference	11
Naming conventions	9
Procurement of technology	9
Technology firm knowledge capture	2
Risk management	14
Standards management	10
Infrastructure architecture	15
Process and service deployment environment	12
Process and service deployment techniques	15
Service catalog management	6
Service management and support	12
Security management	14
Continuous process improvement	9
Costing techniques	8
Strategy management	5
	68.4%

Infrastructure architecture, process and service deployment techniques, control of program, risk management, and security management are cited frequently on the projects, as shown in Table 6.3. Responsibilities and roles, change management, information management, process and service deployment environment, and service management and support are also cited frequently on the projects. Knowledge exchange, common reference, and standards management are cited as enabling in formalizing the methodology on the projects.

Technical Factors

Table 6.4 Key Technical Factors for Enabling Frameworks of Methodology

Technical Factors	Citation Frequency
Internal Web services on project	1
Internal process domain on project	4
Internal SOA domain on project	11
External process domain on project	5
External SOA domain on project	12
Business process management product software	13
Data tools	6
Middleware	12
Platform of key technology firms	13
Platform specialty tools from platform technology firm	11
Proprietary technologies	9
Best-of-class tools	7
XML standard	13
Messaging standards	13
Service description and discovery standards	9
Transaction standards	3
Security standards	9
User interface standards	3
Web services best practices	9
Web services management standards	3
	55.3%

Business process management product software, platforms of key technology firms, XML standard, and messaging standards are cited frequently as enabling technical factors, as shown in Table 6.4. External SOA domain on project and middleware are cited frequently on the projects. Internal SOA domain and platform specialty tools from platform technology firms are cited often on the projects.

These findings of business factors (70.7 percent), and also procedural factors (68.4 percent), as more enabling than technical factors (55.3 percent) in fulfilling SOA may be encouraging for business managerial staff who might be currently hesitant in pursuing SOA as a strategy.

Key Roles of Program Staff

Key roles of the program staff in our studies are executive sponsor and business sponsor from the corporate and business sectors; SOA strategist, communications coordinator, SOA program coordinator, and program methodology specialist from the governance sector; and technical sponsor, infrastructure architect, database analyst, and security specialist from the technology sector. Table 6.5 displays the key roles of program staff.

Table 6.5   Key Roles of Program Staff on SOA

Sector	Citation Frequency
Corporate Sector	
Executive sponsor	4
Business Sector	
Business sponsor	5
Governance Sector	
SOA strategist	8
Communications coordinator	6
SOA program coordinator	5
Program methodology specialist	5
Technology Sector	
Technical sponsor	10
Infrastructure architect	10
Database analyst	8
Security specialist	6

Note: This table displays frequently cited *highest* enabling key roles in each of the sectors from all of the program roles in Tables 3.2, 3.4, 3.6, 3.8, 3.10; 4.2, 4.4, 4.6, 4.8, 4.10, 4.12, 4.14, 4.16; and 5.2 and 5.4 in Chapters 3, 4, and 5, respectively.

The technology sector is cited frequently in technical sponsor, infrastructure architect, database analyst, and security specialist (four key roles in the sector). The governance sector is also cited frequently in SOA strategist, communications coordinator, SOA program coordinator, and program methodology specialist (four key roles), which is encouraging for an enterprise focus of the projects. The business sector and the corporate sector are cited frequently only in business sponsor (one key role) and in executive sponsor, which is not encouraging for business management or client participation on the projects, nor for business SOA strategy, especially as business factors are indicated previously as more enabling than technical factors in fulfilling SOA.

Although roles fulfilled the factors and frameworks of the methodology, they are generally *not* the results of a restructuring of the information technology departments, or of the business units of the firms, into *bona fide* corporate, business, governance, and technical sector teams. The firms in our studies have not evolved fully in a restructuring of organizations and staff but are evolving in SOA. Our feeling is that restructuring is expected to be evident in future studies.

Key Lessons Learned on Projects of SOA

From the bulk of the projects of SOA in our studies, key lessons learned are indicated to exist in close collaboration of staff, enterprise governance of services, evolution of functionality on incremental projects, focus on service standards, and service orientation training, as discussed below:

■ *Close collaboration of the information technology department with the business departments and business units on business requirements can contribute to fast deployment of an SOA solution.* Collaboration and dependence of business units on a technology firm (vendor) without a definition of business process requirements can contribute to slow deployment if not the failure of a project. Collaboration on enterprise architecture requirements, however, may speed deployment of an SOA solution and may not be feasible with business staff.
■ *Enterprise governance of services based on strategic planning can ensure effective and economical reusability of services in an SOA*, especially if governance is centralized in a firm and funded by senior management. Decentralized governance, however, may be a current norm.
■ *Evolution of functionality on incremental projects contributing immediate benefits, in contrast to investment on "big bang" projects contributing elusively later benefits, can be a prudent SOA strategy.* External projects may be more feasible than internal projects, because of less external political constraints. External projects may be possible merely due to more defined external industry standards than internal standards.

- *Focus on service standards at the beginning of a project on SOA can help in creating a solid foundation of SOA solutions and SOA strategy.*
- *Focus on service orientation training of internal technical and business staff from the beginning of a project, and continuous technical training during the projects, are crucial for deployment of an SOA strategy.* Training in the technology departments may be helpful in promoting a culture of innovation in a firm. Internal expertise in an SOA center of competency may help in the training.

Future studies can be expected to disclose further lessons as firms expand experimentation in integration of process and services architecture and in the restructuring of technical and business organizations and staffing.

Maturity of SOA in the Studies

Few of the firms (two) in our studies are close to highest maturity of deployment and exploitation of enterprise services based on SOE. Half (eight) are experimenting in integration of process and services architecture and in restructuring the organizations and teams. Several firms (five) are at a low maturity of department deployment and business unit expansion of Web services based on principles of SOA. Almost all of these firms (thirteen) are achieving competitive equivalency service solutions or competitive continuous improvement service solutions, but the few firms (two) at a high maturity are achieving the *beginning* of competitive differentiation service solutions. Figure 6.1 displays the maturity levels of SOA in the firms in our studies.

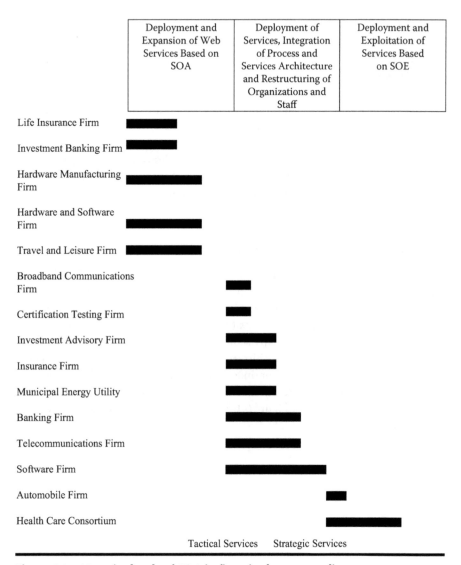

Figure 6.1   Maturity levels of SOA in firms in the case studies.

Future studies of SOA may disclose more achievement in competitive differentiation solutions by all of these firms as they mature with program management methodology in an SOA strategy.

This concludes the methodology section of this book; the next section, Section 3, focuses on technology.

SERVICE-ORIENTED ARCHITECTURE (SOA) TECHNOLOGY

3

The agile enterprise is a journey with no final destination — it is a strategy that will continually impact IT (information technology) … projects.

—**Chip Wilson**
Transparent IT: Building Blocks for an Agile Enterprise[1]

Chapter 7

Introduction to Service Technology

The complexity of service-oriented architecture (SOA) is apparent from the deployments of the business firms in Section 2. Although all the firms have deployed and expanded Web services based on SOA or deployed services, integrated process and services architecture, and restructured organizations and staff, few in the studies have deployed and exploited services based on service-oriented enterprise (SOE). SOA is not easy to develop from the hype of technology firms (vendors) marketing service technology.[2] In our studies, there were collectively different technology firms marketing diverse product technologies and tools, of which the foremost of the firms are indicated in Table 7.1.

The decision on the appropriate technology firm and the best service technology can be difficult for technical managers, and especially for business managers, because of the myriad technology firms and technologies coupled with the immaturity of some of the technologies and the tools.[3]

Difficulty of SOA Technology

The difficulty in SOA, and in general technology,[4] can be addressed both as a challenge and an opportunity for a business firm. Firms must concentrate on the business capabilities and dimensions of SOA, and not on the difficulties of the technology. Business managers, in close collaboration with technical managers in the information technology department, must consider the business needs, the processes that will be improved by SOA, the applications behind the processes, and the core services that will be included in SOA.

Table 7.1   Key SOA Technology Firms in Studies

SOA Technology Firms	
Altova, Inc.	Microsoft Corporation[a]
Amberpoint, Inc.	Oracle[a]
BEA Systems, Inc.[a]	Reactivity
Cape Clear Software, Inc.	Red Hat, Inc.
Hewlett Packard[a]	SOA Software, Inc.[a]
IBM Corporation[a]	Sun Microsystems, Inc.[a]
Informatica Corporation	Tibco Software, Inc.

[a] Firms cited as enabling projects of SOA in multiple case studies of book.

Focus on improvement of business processes is already considered a goal of technical managers.[5] Governance of SOA as a business proposition in improving processes is considered a growing issue for managers.[6] Technology can clearly be difficult for decision makers but it may be a distraction from critical business challenges that could be approached first by technical and business managers.

The evolution of SOA continues to advance with improved functionality of products marketed by technology firms, as large-sized technology firms continue to acquire small-sized firms and hype integrated SOA solutions and suites.[7] Such suites and technologies may be appealing to a business firm but managers and program participants may better evaluate and decide these technologies in contrast to existing internal technologies and levels of services skills of the technical staff, as these might impact the integration of the external suites and technologies. Managers may also best decide to exclude proprietary technologies of technology firms.

The decision on SOA technology is frequently among a number of technology firms, as few technology firms, technologies, and tools are likely to be *the* SOA solution suite, and the decision is appropriate in an SOA that can conveniently integrate diverse and numerous technologies.

The technology firms, technologies, and tools of SOA are furnished as a reference for readers in Chapter 8 on service technology firms, technologies, and tools.

Enterprise Architecture Strategy

The focus on business processes and strategy of SOA can be continued by a concentration on enterprise architecture* before deciding on the technology of SOA.

---

* Application of the Zachman Framework for Enterprise Architecture[9] in the architecture framework of our program management methodology can benefit managers.

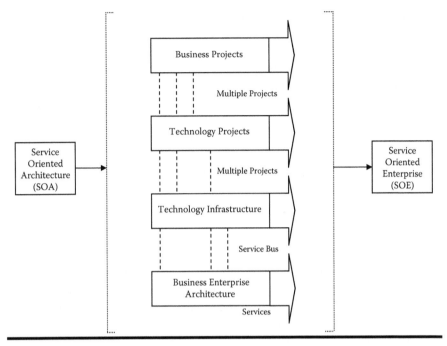

Figure 7.1 Enterprise architecture strategy.

The architecture is a blueprint of the dimensions of flexible services that can deliver the improved processes, as conceptually displayed in Figure 7.1. The architecture describes business logic, data management, access control criteria, interface, messaging and organization of applications, and metadata of applications of future services and existing services, enabling eventual infrastructure and process standardization throughout the business units of the firm in an SOE. The metadata is the glue to the properties of the business processes. Description of the processes and the architecture is in business terminology. Such dimensions of enterprise architecture do not depend on specific technologies.

Architecture is the foundation of SOA strategy and is effectively independent of the technology. To benefit from an SOA, the focus of managers must be on business processes and on an enterprise architecture plan, and not purely on the technologies.[8]

This plan can include recommendations for integration of legacy applications in an SOA. Managers might integrate legacy applications in an enterprise service bus (ESB) from a technology firm. The bus is essentially a messaging bus and a platform for orchestrating and provisioning services. An example of a project with an ESB is the municipal energy utility in Case Study 10 in Chapter 5, but another example might be order processing of securities, which has complex procedures and requires synchronization of transactions. Managers might alternately not integrate applications in an ESB, which is akin to enterprise application integration (EAI); they might interface them in XML gateways to the services, as interfaces are likely more loosely coupled and dynamically linked to applications than integration. The plan for infrastructure architecture may likely recommend a number of technology options that would be included in the SOA strategy.

Other issues include the performance and the scalability of the architecture, which may negate the benefits of SOA, and on which the focus of managers in specifying performance and scalability requirements are more important than the inherent technologies of the technology firms.

The decision on investment in technology of SOA is subordinate to enterprise architecture and business process strategy.

Security of SOA

Although the focus on business processes and enterprise architecture strategy is critical in an SOA, managers in the technology department must consider the dimensions of the security of services and of SOA before deciding on the technology firms, their technologies, and the tools.

The ease in exposing internal applications and furnishing core services to internal and external consumers and intermediaries causes concerns for a business firm.[10] Securing services is a critical consideration for managers and program participants evaluating products of technology firms.

To ensure security of SOA, access control to services, authorization to the services, and authentication of authorized consumers for specific services can be designed by managers and staff, defined in a security policy during the initiation of projects, and modified by the staff during product realization.

Managers might develop procedures from a Web Services Description Language (WSDL) design to ensure that affected applications and all services of the firm are enabled by security from the design. They might develop common security for all the applications and the services for all the consumers in the firm, distinct security for designated application domains or for designated services for designated internal consumers in the firm, and exception security for services for consumers in external firms and for individual customers. To do this, they might merge the SOA security policy with existing practices on security and not have conflicting security.

The design of procedures of a security policy can be done during the gathering of technical and business requirements for services. Managers and staff might consider the existing functionality of marketplace security tools as they design a security policy and then decide on the tools of a technology firm. The management of the policy and of the security technologies and the tools of the technology firms is important in SOA strategy.[11]

Standards of SOA

The difficulty of SOA in different technology firms and numerous product technologies is exacerbated by Web services standards. To evolve from Web services to SOA, requirements have expanded for extension to existing standards. The specifications on the technologies and the tools are developed generally by groups of large-sized technology firms, such as BEA, IBM, Microsoft, SAP, and Tibco,[12] and are forwarded by them to one or more of the foremost organizations[13] on standards indicated in Table 7.2. Following a review process, specifications may or may not be approved as standards, or the specifications may expire prior to approval. Technology firms, however, may develop and market products that adhere to specifications that are not approved as standards, further exacerbating difficulties.

Other organizations important in standards include the Association for Cooperative Operations Research and Development (ACORD), the Financial Services Technology Consortium (FSTC), the Interactive Financial Exchange (IFX), the Liberty Alliance, and the United Nations Centre for Trade Facilitation and Electronic Business (UN/CEFACT).

The organizations in Table 7.2 are cross-referenced to current standards in Table 7.3.

The technology firms are evolving generally to common open standards, but current standards displayed in Table 7.3 are conflicting and overlapping, and it can be difficult for managers in a business firm to choose appropriate standards.

Managers may discover that features in the simple Web services specifications of the standards may be adequate for their firms, but may find that a few of the functions in the extended SOA standards may be inadequate for several specific applications in the firms. An example of an application might be a designated service

Table 7.2   Key SOA Standards Organizations

SOA Standards Organizations
Business Process Management Initiative (BPMI)
Internet Engineering Task Force (IETF)
Java Community Process (JCP)
Object Management Group (OMG)
Organization for the Advancement of Structured Information Standards (OASIS)
Web Services Interoperability (WS-I)
World Wide Web Consortium (W3C)

Table 7.3 Key SOA Standards Organizations and Standards

Layer of Services	Standards	Standards Organizations
Management		
SPML	Service Provisioning Markup Language	OASIS OMG
WS-DM	Distributed Management[a]	OASIS
WS-F	Federation	Consortium of technology firms
WS-I	Interoperability[a]	WS-I
WS-Policy		W3C
WS-Provisioning		OASIS
Presentation		
WS-RP	Remote Portlets	OASIS
WSXL	Experience Language	IBM OASIS
Process		
BPML	Business Process Modeling Language	BPMI OMG
BPMN	Business Process Modeling Notation	BPMI OMG
BPQL	Business Process Query Language	BPMI OMG
ebXML	Electronic Business eXtensible Markup Language	OASIS UN/CEFACT
WS-BPEL	Business Process Execution Language[a]	OASIS
WS-C	Choreography	W3C
WS-CAF	Composite Application Framework	OASIS
WSCL	Conversation Language	W3C
WSFL	Flow Language	W3C

Table 7.3 (continued) Key SOA Standards Organizations and Standards

Layer of Services	Standards	Standards Organizations
Session		
WS-RF	Resource Framework	OASIS
Transaction		
WS-AT	Atomic Transaction	OASIS
WS-CDL	Choreography Description Language	W3C
WS-RF	Resource Framework	OASIS
WS-Transfer		W3C
WS-TX	Transaction	OASIS
Invocation		
JAX-RPC	Java API [Application Program Interface] for XML Remote Procedure Call	JCP
WS-E	Eventing	W3C
WSIF	Invocation Framework	JCP
WS-N	Notification	OASIS
Description and Discovery		
UDDI	Universal Description, Discovery and Integration[a]	OASIS
WSDL	Description Language[a]	OMG W3C
WSIL	Inspection Language	IBM Microsoft
Publication		
UDDI	Universal Description, Discovery and Integration[a]	OASIS
WS-Metadata Exchange		Consortium of technology firms

Table 7.3 (continued)   Key SOA Standards Organizations and Standards

Layer of Services	Standards	Standards Organizations
Security		
SAML	Security Assertions Markup Language	OASIS
WS-S	Security[a]	OASIS
WS-SC	Secure Conversation	OASIS
WS-SP	Security Policy	OASIS
WS-Trust		OASIS
XML	Encryption[a]	W3C
XML	Signature[a]	IETF W3C
Messaging		
ASAP	Asynchronous Service Access Protocol	OASIS
SOAP	Simple Object Access Protocol[a]	W3C
SOAP MTOM	Message Transmission Optimization Mechanism	W3C
SWA	SOAP Attachments	W3C
Transport		
BEEP	Block Extensible Exchange Protocol	IETF
WS-R	Reliability	OASIS
WS-RM	Reliable Messaging[a]	OASIS
Protocol		
FTP	File Transfer Protocol	IETF
HTTP	Hypertext Transfer Protocol[a]	IETF W3C
SMTP	Simple Mail Transfer Protocol	IETF

Note: Descriptions of the standards are in Chapter 10 on service terminology.

[a] Standards integrated in projects of SOA in case studies of book.

for designated external business firms that cannot be published without further security. Managers might not have technology-neutral services, due to legacy applications developed in closed proprietary protocols and technologies. They might be impacted by technology firms tightly coupling their software, so that they are effectively furnishing closed proprietary technologies. Such issues indicate the immaturity of the specification standards and the technologies.

To decide on a standards strategy, given the issues, managers and program participants can first determine business needs, choose products that address these needs, and ascertain that the products adhere to approved specifications or standards. Managers can ascertain that previously purchased products from different technology firms conform to the same standards. They can focus on the best-of-class technologies and tools of the large-sized technology firms that dominate the standards, in an effort to continue deploying initial services in SOA. However, managers must consider matured and open specification standards of SOA technologies as a preferred requirement for technology firms, so as to enable a more stable foundation for the future growth of SOA. Technology firms committed to open standards and standard interoperability techniques enable an appropriate business and management strategy of SOA.

Version Control

The final difficulty in the management of SOA is version control of the services and of the product technologies and synchronization between technologies and versions of the services. Business firms continue to deploy more and more services and may have multiple versions of the same services, and technology firms continue to deploy numerous releases of their technologies. Managers can have difficulty maintaining *bona fide* reusability of the services, due to shifting of the technologies and the services.

Managers might map common consumer calls for a new service to an old service in a translation service if data for the new service could be derived for the service in the translation. Management of the services and of the technologies is better in a policy aided by a registry or a repository containing characteristics of the services, standards, and technologies and customized to the requirements of their firms. Multiple service versions may be included in a registry with cross-referencing between providers and consumers of the services. Service metadata with versions of product technologies that created the services may be further included in the registry. The registry would facilitate testing of related applications when services are updated and of related services when technologies are upgraded in the firms, to ensure changes in versions are not introducing new problems. Such a policy is important in version control of SOA strategy, as indicated in the service management framework of the program management methodology in Chapter 2 and in a number of our studies.

In short, the management of SOA technology, and of enterprise architecture strategy, security, standards, and version control of services and technologies can be Herculean for technical managers and business managers. Nevertheless, managers can collaborate on the capabilities and deployment methods of new technologies,[14] and influence and lead projects of SOA on the path to an eventual SOE. SOA is considered an organic process requiring participation of business stakeholder staff and technology staff for the duration and evolution of the projects and in the decisions on service firms, technologies, and tools,[15] which are categorized in Chapter 8.

Notes

1. Wilson, C. 2006. *Transparent IT: Building Blocks for an Agile Enterprise.* Geniant, LLC, Dallas, TX, p. 187.
2. Fitzgerald, M. 2006. Getting Good Service. *CIO Insight,* October, p. 74.
3. Whiting, R. 2006. SOA Toolbox Still Is Not Full. *Information Week,* October 9, p. 27–28.
4. McAfee, A. 2006. Mastering the Three Worlds of Information Technology. *Harvard Business Review,* November, p. 142.
5. Alter, A. 2006. Top 30 Trends for 2007: Process Improvement Will Be Job No. 1. *CIO Insight,* December, p. 12.
6. Knorr, E. 2007. SOA: The Great SOA Shopping Spree. *Infoworld,* January 1, p. 16.
7. Koch, C. 2006. Service-Oriented Architecture: The Truth About SOA. *CIO,* June 15, p. 58.
8. Gruman, G. 2006. True Challenge of SOA — It Is Not Technology. *CIO,* May 1, p. 25.
9. O'Rourke, C., Fishman, N., and Selkow, W. 2003. *Enterprise Architecture Using the Zachman Framework (MIS).* Thomson Course Technology, Boston, MA.
10. Goodin, D. 2006. Shielding Web Services from Attack. *Infoworld,* November 27, p. 29.
11. Linthicum, D. 2007. Budgeting for SOA Success. *Infoworld,* January 8, p. 20.
12. Newcomer, E. and Lomow, G. 2005. *Understanding SOA with Web Services.* Addison-Wesley, Upper Saddle River, NJ, p. 33.
13. Newcomer and Lomow, *Understanding SOA with Web Services,* p. 33–34.
14. McAfee, A. 2006. Mastering the Three Worlds of Information Technology. *Harvard Business Review,* November, p. 147.
15. Fox, S. 2006. Sustainable SOA. *Infoworld,* May 8, p. 6.

Chapter 8

Service Technology Firms, Technologies, and Tools

This chapter distinguishes SOA technology firms (vendors) by technologies and tools, as they are applied in the frameworks of our program management methodology. We include information on the firms to enable readers to contact them for further information. The chapter lists other research sources on SOA technology to facilitate follow-up on the state of SOA technologies and trends.

SOA Technology Firms

As discussed in Chapter 7, the challenge in SOA technology lies in the multiple numbers of technology firms marketing numerous technologies.

Business firms having complex integration requirements for heterogeneous groups of internal and external applications may need a number of SOA product technologies and tools that can come from a number of technology firms. Large-sized and medium-sized business firms might depend on SOA technologies and specialty tools from only the platform of a key technology firm (e.g., IBM or Microsoft), but alternately might depend on the key technology firm for the bulk of SOA technologies and on other technology firms (e.g., AmberPoint, Cape Clear, or EMC) for best-of-class specialty tools, which was evident frequently in the studies. Small-sized business firms having simple integration requirements for a homogeneous infrastructure of internal applications on a platform of the key technology firm may not need SOA technology.

The decision on technology firms and the technologies depends on the technical conditions and, of course, upon the business criteria and strategy of the business firms.

Because the decision on SOA technology also depends on requirements, Table 8.1 provides the scope of the technologies and tools as they may be applied in

Table 8.1   Service Technologies and Tools

Service Technologies and Tools	Frameworks of Methodology								
	Governance	Communications	Product Realization	Project Management	Architecture	Data Management	Service Management	Human Resource Management	Post Implementation
Application integration and legacy adaptation			■						■
Asset inventory management			■				■		
Business process management and modeling			■				■		■
Configuration and deployment management			■		■				
Data management and transformation			■			■	■		■
Development, integration, and service			■				■		
Knowledge management	■	■	■	■	■	■	■		■
Management and monitoring	■	■							■
Middleware and service bus					■				■
Networking					■				■
Registry and repository	■	■	■				■		■
Run time					■				■
Security					■				■
Testing			■						

the frameworks of our program management methodology, based on distinct SOA maturity scenarios.

Clearly, a diversity of technologies and tools from one technology firm or a number of firms is required in a matured SOA solution, and Table 8.2 displays these technology firms by the technologies and tools, as applied again in our methodology.

Technologies conforming to nonproprietary standards are critical criteria in the decisions on these technology firms, as SOA moves the industry toward more open standards.

Table 8.3 provides further information on the technology firms for reference and specific inquiry on these technologies and tools.

To follow up on the state of SOA technology, we list recent research sources that may be helpful to readers.

Table 8.2 Service Technology Firms, Technologies, and Tools

Service Technologies and Tools	Frameworks of Methodology								
	Governance	*Communications*	*Product Realization*	*Project Management*	*Architecture*	*Data Management*	*Service Management*	*Human Resource Management*	*Post Implementation*
Application Integration and Legacy Adaptation			■						■
Adeptia			■						■
Attachmate			■						■
Axway Cyclone			■						■
BEA Systems[a]			■						■
Brixlogic			■						■
Business Integration			■						■
Cordys America			■						■
Denodo Technologies			■						■
E2E Technologies			■						■
Fiorano Software			■						■

Table 8.2 (continued)   Service Technology Firms, Technologies, and Tools

Service Technologies and Tools	Frameworks of Methodology								
	Governance	Communications	Product Realization	Project Management	Architecture	Data Management	Service Management	Human Resource Management	Post Implementation
Fujitsu			■						■
GridScope			■						■
HandySoft Global			■						■
HostBridge Technology			■						■
IBM[a]			■						■
Intel			■						■
Intersystems			■						■
IONA Technologies			■						■
Ipedo			■						■
iWay Sify			■						■
JackBe			■						■
Jitterbit			■						■
Kingdee International			■						■
Micro Focus			■						■
OpenLink Software			■						■
Progress Software			■						■
RatchetSoft			■						■
Real-Time Innovations			■						■
Rearden Commerce			■						■
Recursion Software			■						■
Rogue Wave Software			■						■

Table 8.2 (continued)   Service Technology Firms, Technologies, and Tools

Service Technologies and Tools	Frameworks of Methodology								
	Governance	Communications	Product Realization	Project Management	Architecture	Data Management	Service Management	Human Resource Management	Post Implementation
SOA Software[a]			■						■
Sun Microsystems[a]			■						■
webMethods			■						■
Xcalia USA			■						■
Asset Inventory Management			■				■		
BEA Systems[a]			■				■		
BluePhoenix			■				■		
Borland Software			■				■		
Majitek Pty			■				■		
Business Process Management and Modeling			■				■		■
Adeptia			■				■		■
Adobe Systems			■				■		■
Appian			■				■		■
Active EndPoints			■				■		■
Axway Cyclone			■				■		■
BEA Systems[a]			■				■		■
BusinessGenetics			■				■		■
Cordys America			■				■		■
Corel			■				■		■
E2E Technologies			■				■		■

Table 8.2 (continued)   Service Technology Firms, Technologies, and Tools

Service Technologies and Tools	Frameworks of Methodology								
	Governance	Communications	Product Realization	Project Management	Architecture	Data Management	Service Management	Human Resource Management	Post Implementation
EMC[a]			■				■		■
Engineous Software			■				■		■
Fiorano Software			■				■		■
Fujitsu			■				■		■
Global 360			■				■		■
HandySoft Global			■				■		■
IBM[a]			■				■		■
IDS Scheer			■				■		■
Intalio			■				■		■
Intersystems			■				■		■
iWay Sify			■				■		■
Jacada			■				■		■
JackBe			■				■		■
Lombardi Software			■				■		■
Magic Software			■				■		■
Metastorm			■				■		■
Microsoft[a]			■				■		■
Novell			■				■		■
OpenLink Software			■				■		■
OpenStorm Software			■				■		■
Oracle[a]			■				■		■

Table 8.2 (continued)   Service Technology Firms, Technologies, and Tools

Service Technologies and Tools	Frameworks of Methodology								
	Governance	*Communications*	*Product Realization*	*Project Management*	*Architecture*	*Data Management*	*Service Management*	*Human Resource Management*	*Post Implementation*
OW2			■				■		■
Parasoft			■				■		■
Pegasystems			■				■		■
Progress Software			■				■		■
ReadiMinds Systems			■				■		■
Red Hat[a]			■				■		■
SAP America			■				■		■
Savvion			■				■		■
Select Business Solutions			■				■		■
Singularity			■				■		■
Skelta Software			■				■		■
Software AG			■				■		■
SourceCode Technology			■				■		■
Sun Microsystems[a]			■				■		■
Telelogic			■				■		■
Ultimus			■				■		■
Vitria Technology			■				■		■
webMethods			■				■		■
WebV2			■				■		■
Configuration and Deployment Management			■		■				

Table 8.2 (continued)   Service Technology Firms, Technologies, and Tools

Service Technologies and Tools	Governance	Communications	Product Realization	Project Management	Architecture	Data Management	Service Management	Human Resource Management	Post Implementation
					Frameworks of Methodology				
BluePhoenix			■		■				
Borland Software			■		■				
Cincom Systems			■		■				
IBM[a]			■		■				
Majitek Pty			■		■				
OpenCloud			■		■				
Pramati Technologies			■		■				
Telelogic			■		■				
WebLayers			■		■				
Zend Technologies			■		■				
Data Management and Transformation			■			■	■		■
Adeptia			■			■	■		■
Apache Software			■			■	■		■
Autonomy			■			■	■		■
Axway Cyclone			■			■	■		■
BluePhoenix			■			■	■		■
Brixlogic			■			■	■		■
Cape Clear Software[a]			■			■	■		■
Cincom Systems			■			■	■		■
ClearNova			■			■	■		■

Table 8.2 (continued)   Service Technology Firms, Technologies, and Tools

Service Technologies and Tools	Governance	Communications	Product Realization	Project Management	Architecture	Data Management	Service Management	Human Resource Management	Post Implementation
			Frameworks of Methodology						
Cordys America			■			■	■		■
Countermind			■			■	■		■
Data Direct Technologies			■			■	■		■
Denodo Technologies			■			■	■		■
EMC[a]			■			■	■		■
Fujitsu			■			■	■		■
Gemstone			■			■	■		■
Gigaspaces			■			■	■		■
HandySoft Global			■			■	■		■
HostBridge Technology			■			■	■		■
IBM[a]			■			■	■		■
Informatica[a]			■			■	■		■
Intersystems			■			■	■		■
Ipedo			■			■	■		■
Jitterbit			■			■	■		■
Layer 7 Technologies			■			■	■		■
OpenLink Software			■			■	■		■
OW2			■			■	■		■
Progress Software			■			■	■		■
Red Hat[a]			■			■	■		■
Scientio			■			■	■		■

Table 8.2 (continued)   Service Technology Firms, Technologies, and Tools

Service Technologies and Tools	Frameworks of Methodology								
	Governance	*Communications*	*Product Realization*	*Project Management*	*Architecture*	*Data Management*	*Service Management*	*Human Resource Management*	*Post Implementation*
Select Business Solutions			◼			◼	◼		◼
Tarari			◼			◼	◼		◼
webMethods			◼			◼	◼		◼
XAware			◼			◼	◼		◼
Development, Integration and Service			◼				◼		
Altova[a]			◼				◼		
Apache Software			◼				◼		
Attachmate			◼				◼		
BEA Systems[a]			◼				◼		
BluePhoenix			◼				◼		
Borland Software			◼				◼		
Brixlogic			◼				◼		
Caucho Technology			◼				◼		
Cincom Systems			◼				◼		
ClearNova			◼				◼		
Cordys America			◼				◼		
Countermind			◼				◼		
Data Direct Technologies			◼				◼		
EMC[a]			◼				◼		
Exaltec Software			◼				◼		

Table 8.2 (continued)   Service Technology Firms, Technologies, and Tools

Service Technologies and Tools	Governance	Communications	Product Realization	Project Management	Architecture	Data Management	Service Management	Human Resource Management	Post Implementation
			Frameworks of Methodology						
Fujitsu			■				■		
HandySoft Global			■				■		
IBM[a]			■				■		
ILog			■				■		
Intersystems			■				■		
IONA Technologies			■				■		
Ipedo			■				■		
JackBe			■				■		
Jitterbit			■				■		
Kingdee International			■				■		
Magic Software			■				■		
Majitek Pty			■				■		
Micro Focus			■				■		
Microsoft[a]			■				■		
mobicents.dev.java.net			■				■		
OpenCloud			■				■		
OpenConnect Systems			■				■		
Oracle[a]			■				■		
OW2			■				■		
Pramati Technologies			■				■		
Real-Time Innovations			■				■		

Table 8.2 (continued) Service Technology Firms, Technologies, and Tools

Service Technologies and Tools	Governance	Communications	Product Realization	Project Management	Architecture	Data Management	Service Management	Human Resource Management	Post Implementation
Recursa Software			■				■		
Recursion Software			■				■		
Red Hat[a]			■				■		
Relativity Technologies			■				■		
Seagull Software Systems			■				■		
Seapine Software			■				■		
Select Business Solutions			■				■		
Servoy			■				■		
Software AG			■				■		
StrikeIron			■				■		
Sun Microsystems[a]			■				■		
Synergy Financial			■				■		
Telelogic			■				■		
Tibco Software[a]			■				■		
WebCollage USA			■				■		
WebLayers			■				■		
webMethods			■				■		
XAware			■				■		
Xcalia USA			■				■		
Zend Technologies			■				■		
Knowledge Management	■	■	■	■	■	■	■		■

The columns are grouped under the heading *Frameworks of Methodology*.

Table 8.2 (continued) Service Technology Firms, Technologies, and Tools

Service Technologies and Tools	Governance	Communications	Product Realization	Project Management	Architecture	Data Management	Service Management	Human Resource Management	Post Implementation
	Frameworks of Methodology								
Adobe Systems	■	■	■	■	■	■	■		■
Apache Software	■	■	■	■	■	■	■		■
Appian	■	■	■	■	■	■	■		■
Axway Cyclone	■	■	■	■	■	■	■		■
Borland Software	■	■	■	■	■	■	■		■
Cincom Systems	■	■	■	■	■	■	■		■
EMC[a]	■	■	■	■	■	■	■		■
Global 360	■	■	■	■	■	■	■		■
IBM[a]	■	■	■	■	■	■	■		■
iWay Sify	■	■	■	■	■	■	■		■
Miro	■	■	■	■	■	■	■		■
Oracle[a]	■	■	■	■	■	■	■		■
Relativity Technologies	■	■	■	■	■	■	■		■
Management and Monitoring	■	■							■
Amberpoint[a]	■	■							■
Cape Clear Software[a]	■	■							■
Computer Associates	■	■							■
Cordys America	■	■							■
Countermind	■	■							■
Fujitsu	■	■							■
GridScope	■	■							■

Table 8.2 (continued)   Service Technology Firms, Technologies, and Tools

Service Technologies and Tools	Governance	Communications	Product Realization	Project Management	Architecture	Data Management	Service Management	Human Resource Management	Post Implementation
HandySoft Global	■	■							■
Hewlett Packard*	■	■							■
IBM[a]	■	■							■
IDS Scheer	■	■							■
Infravio	■	■							■
Intalio	■	■							■
Integrasolv	■	■							■
Itellix Software	■	■							■
iWay Sify	■	■							■
Jitterbit	■	■							■
Layer 7 Technologies	■	■							■
Majitek Pty	■	■							■
Managed Methods	■	■							■
Mindreef	■	■							■
mobicents.dev.java.net	■	■							■
OpenConnect Systems	■	■							■
Oracle[a]	■	■							■
OW2	■	■							■
ReadiMinds Systems	■	■							■
SOA Software[a]	■	■							■
SourceCode Technology	■	■							■

The column headers "Governance" through "Post Implementation" fall under the grouping **Frameworks of Methodology**.

Table 8.2 (continued)   Service Technology Firms, Technologies, and Tools

Service Technologies and Tools	Frameworks of Methodology								
	Governance	*Communications*	*Product Realization*	*Project Management*	*Architecture*	*Data Management*	*Service Management*	*Human Resource Management*	*Post Implementation*
Sun Microsystems[a]	■	■							■
Tibco Software[a]	■	■							■
WebLayers	■	■							■
webMethods	■	■							■
WestGlobal	■	■							■
Xcalia USA	■	■							■
Middleware and Service Bus					■				■
Apache Software					■				■
Appligent					■				■
Axway Cyclone					■				■
BEA Systems[a]					■				■
Borland Software					■				■
Brixlogic					■				■
Business Integration					■				■
Cape Clear Software[a]					■				■
Cordys America					■				■
Data Direct Technologies					■				■
Denodo Technologies					■				■
E2E Technologies					■				■
Fiorano Software					■				■
Fujitsu					■				■

Table 8.2 (continued)   Service Technology Firms, Technologies, and Tools

Service Technologies and Tools	Governance	Communications	Product Realization	Project Management	Architecture	Data Management	Service Management	Human Resource Management	Post Implementation
	Frameworks of Methodology								
GridScope					■				■
IBM[a]					■				■
Intel					■				■
IONA Technologies					■				■
iWay Sify					■				■
JackBe					■				■
Layer 7 Technologies					■				■
Logic Blaze					■				■
Majitek Pty					■				■
Managed Methods					■				■
Oracle[a]					■				■
OW2					■				■
Progress Software					■				■
Real-Time Innovations					■				■
Recursion Software					■				■
Red Hat[a]					■				■
SOA Software[a]					■				■
Sonic Software					■				■
Xcalia USA					■				■
Networking					■				■
Accordare					■				■

Table 8.2 (continued)   Service Technology Firms, Technologies, and Tools

Service Technologies and Tools	*Governance*	*Communications*	*Product Realization*	*Project Management*	*Architecture*	*Data Management*	*Service Management*	*Human Resource Management*	*Post Implementation*
					Frameworks of Methodology				
Azul Systems					■				■
Business Integration					■				■
Cisco Systems					■				■
Fujitsu					■				■
Jnetx					■				■
OpenCloud					■				■
Registry and Repository	■	■	■				■		■
Apache Software	■	■	■				■		■
GridScope	■	■	■				■		■
HandySoft Global	■	■	■				■		■
Hewlett Packard[a]	■	■	■				■		■
IBM[a]	■	■	■				■		■
Infravio	■	■	■				■		■
Oracle[a]	■	■	■				■		■
SOA Software	■	■	■				■		■
Software AG	■	■	■				■		■
Run Time					■				■
Apache Software					■				■
Appistry					■				■
Azul Systems					■				■
BEA Systems[a]					■				■

Table 8.2 (continued)   Service Technology Firms, Technologies, and Tools

Service Technologies and Tools	Frameworks of Methodology								
	Governance	*Communications*	*Product Realization*	*Project Management*	*Architecture*	*Data Management*	*Service Management*	*Human Resource Management*	*Post Implementation*
Borland Software					■				■
Caucho Technology					■				■
Cordys America					■				■
Countermind					■				■
Data Direct Technologies					■				■
Fiorano Software					■				■
Fujitsu					■				■
Gigaspaces					■				■
IBM[a]					■				■
Intel					■				■
Jnetx					■				■
Kabira Technologies					■				■
Logic Blaze					■				■
Majitek Pty					■				■
Managed Methods					■				■
Microsoft[a]					■				■
mobicents.dev.java.net					■				■
Novell					■				■
OW2					■				■
Pramati Technologies					■				■
Recursion Software					■				■

Table 8.2 (continued)   Service Technology Firms, Technologies, and Tools

Service Technologies and Tools	Frameworks of Methodology								
	Governance	Communications	Product Realization	Project Management	Architecture	Data Management	Service Management	Human Resource Management	Post Implementation
Red Hat[a]					■				■
Servoy					■				■
Verari Systems					■				■
XAware					■				■
Xcalia USA					■				■
Zend Technologies					■				■
Security					■				■
Apache Software					■				■
BEA Systems[a]					■				■
Cape Clear Software[a]					■				■
Citrix Systems					■				■
Computer Associates					■				■
Cordys America					■				■
Countermind					■				■
EMC[a]					■				■
Forum Systems					■				■
Fujitsu					■				■
IBM[a]					■				■
Intel					■				■
JackBe					■				■
Layer 7 Technologies					■				■

Table 8.2 (continued)   Service Technology Firms, Technologies, and Tools

Service Technologies and Tools	Governance	Communications	Product Realization	Project Management	Architecture	Data Management	Service Management	Human Resource Management	Post Implementation
					Frameworks of Methodology				
Majitek Pty					■				■
Managed Methods					■				■
Progress Software					■				■
Reactivity[a]					■				■
Safelayer					■				■
SOA Software[a]					■				■
Sun Microsystems[a]					■				■
Symantec					■				■
Vordel					■				■
Xcalia USA					■				■
Testing			■						
Apache Software			■						
Borland Software			■						
Cincom Systems			■						
HandySoft Global			■						
Hewlett Packard[a]			■						
IBM[a]			■						
iTKO			■						
Mindreef			■						
Parasoft			■						
Pramati Technologies			■						

Table 8.2 (continued)   Service Technology Firms, Technologies, and Tools

Service Technologies and Tools	Frameworks of Methodology								
	Governance	Communications	Product Realization	Project Management	Architecture	Data Management	Service Management	Human Resource Management	Post Implementation
Seapine Software			■						
Solstice Software			■						
Telelogic			■						
Pramati Technologies			■						
Seapine Software			■						
Telelogic			■						

[a] Firms enabling projects of SOA in case studies of this book.

Table 8.3   Service Technology Firms

Accordare, Inc.
www.accordare.com
info@accordare.com
27 Ashland Street
Arlington, Massachusetts 02476
781-646-2241 (Telephone)
781-646-2242 (Fax)

Active EndPoints, Inc.
www.active-endpoints.com
info@active-endpoints.com
Three Enterprise Drive, Suite 411
Shelton, Connecticut 06484
203-929-9400 (Telephone)
203-929-9429 (Fax)

Adeptia, Inc.
www.adeptia.com
webmaster@adeptia.com
443 North Clark Avenue, Suite 350
Chicago, Illinois 60610
312-229-1727 (Telephone)
312-229-1736 (Fax)

Adobe Systems, Inc.
www.adobe.com
345 Park Avenue
San Jose, California 95110-2704
408-536-6000 (Telephone)
408-537-6000 (Fax)

Table 8.3 (continued)   Service Technology Firms

Altova, Inc.*
www.altova.com
us-sales@altova.com
900 Cummings Center, Suite 314 T
Beverly, Massachusetts 01915-6181
978-816-1600 (Telephone)
1-978-816-1606 (Fax)

Amberpoint, Inc.*
www.amberpoint.com
info@amberpoint.com
155 Grand Avenue, Suite 404
Oakland, California 94612
510-663-6300 (Telephone)
510-663-6301 (Fax)

Apache Software Foundation
www.apache.org
1901 Munsey Drive
Forest Hill, Maryland 21050
410-803-2258 (Fax)

Appian Corporation
www.appian.com
info@appian.com
8000 Towers Crescent Drive, 16th
  Floor
Vienna, Virginia 22182
703-442-8844 (Telephone)
703-442-8919 (Fax)

Appistry, Inc.
www.appistry.com
One City Place Drive, Suite 470
St. Louis, Missouri 63141
314-336-5080 (Telephone)
314-336-5086 (Fax)

Appligent, Inc.
www.appligent.com
support@appligent.com
22 East Baltimore Avenue
Lansdowne, Pennsylvania 19050
610-284-4006 (Telephone)
610-284-4233 (Fax)

Attachmate Corporation
www.attachmate.com
1500 Dexter Avenue N
Seattle, Washington 98109
206-217-7100 (Telephone)
800-872-2829 (Telephone)
206-217-7515 (Fax)

Autonomy, Inc.
www.autonomy.com
autonomy@autonomy.com
One Market Plaza, 19th Floor
Spear Tower
San Francisco, California 94105
415-243-9955 (Telephone)
415-243-9984 (Fax)

Axway Cyclone Commerce
www.axway.com
8388 East Hartford Drive
Scottsdale, Arizona 85255
480-627-1800 (Telephone)
480-627-1801 (Fax)

Azul Systems, Inc.
www.azulsystems.com
info@azulsystems.com
1600 Plymouth Street
Mountain View, California 94043
650-230-6500 (Telephone)
650-230-6600 (Fax)

BEA Systems, Inc.*
www.bea.com/soa
2315 North First Street
San Jose, California 95131
408-570-8000 (Telephone)
800-817-4BEA (Telephone)
408-570-8071 (Fax)

BluePhoenix Solutions
www.bluephoenixsolutions.com
usa@bphx.com
8000 Regency Parkway, Suite 300
Cary, North Carolina 27518

Table 8.3 (continued)   Service Technology Firms

919-380-5100 (Telephone)
919-380-5111 (Fax)

Borland Software Corporation
www.borland.com
20450 Stevens Creek Boulevard,
 Suite 800
Cupertino, California
408-863-2800 (Telephone)

Brixlogic Inc.
www.brixlogic.com
contact-us@brixlogic.com
1660 South Amphlett Boulevard,
 Suite 202
San Mateo, California 94402
650-638-7802 (Telephone)

Business Integration Technology
www.BusinessIntegrationTechnology.
 com
info@BusinessIntegrationTechnology.
 com
1306 Papin Street
St. Louis, Missouri 63103
314-635-6351 (Telephone)
314-256-9214 (Fax)

BusinessGenetics
www.businessgenetics.com
9605 South Kingston Court,
 Suite 290
Englewood, Colorado 80112
720-266-1024 (Telephone)

Cape Clear Software, Inc.*
www.capeclear.com
info@capeclear.com   .
1900 South Norfolk Street, Suite 305
San Mateo, California 94403
650-572-2200 (Telephone)
650-572-2201 (Fax)

Caucho Technology, Inc.
www.caucho.com
sales@caucho.com

San Diego, California
858-456-0300 (Telephone)
858-777-3636 (Fax)

Cincom Systems
www.swiftwebtechnologies.com
info@swiftwebtechnologies.com
2324 Deveron Drive
Louisville, Kentucky 40216
502-449-9953 (Telephone)

Cisco Systems, Inc.
www.cisco.com
170 West Tasman Drive
San Jose, California 95134-1706
408-526-4000 (Telephone)
800-553-6387 (Telephone)
408-526-4100 (Fax)

Citrix Systems, Inc.
www.teros.com
851 West Cypress Creek Road
Fort Lauderdale, Florida 33309
954-267-3000 (Telephone)
800-424-8749 (Telephone)
954-267-9319 (Fax)

ClearNova, Inc.
www.clearnova.com
info@clearnova.com
1150 North Meadow Parkway,
 Suite 118
Roswell, Georgia 30076
770-442-8324 (Telephone)
877-223-8651 (Telephone)
770-442-5975 (Fax)

Computer Associates (CA), Inc.
www.computerassociates.com
One CA Plaza
Islandia, New York 11749
631-342-6000 (Telephone)
800-225-5224 (Telephone)
631-342-6800 (Fax)

Table 8.3 (continued)   Service Technology Firms

Cordys America
www.cordys.com
info-america@cordys.com
1875 South Grant Street, Suite 910
San Mateo, California 94402-2671
650-358-1030 (Telephone)

Corel Corporation
www.corel.com
1600 Carling Avenue
Ottawa, Ontario, Canada K1Z 8R7
800-772-6735 (Telephone)

Countermind, LLC
www.countermind.com
info@countermind.com
1420 West Canal Court, Suite 20
Littleton, Colorado 80120
303-794-1628 (Telephone)
720-407-0213 (Telephone)

DataDirect Technologies
www.shadowRTE.com
support@neonsys.com
1500 Perimeter Park Drive, Suite 100
Morrisville, North Carolina 27560
919-461-4200 (Telephone)
800-876-3101
919-461-4529 (Fax)

Denodo Technologies Americas
www.denodo.com
530 Lytton Avenue, Suite 302
Palo Alto, California 94301
650-566-8833 (Telephone)
650-566-8836 (Fax)

E2E Technologies, Ltd.
www.e2ebridge.com
dfrisoli@e2ebridge.com
312 Stuart Street
Boston, Massachusetts 02216
617-421-4431 (Telephone)
617-960-3535 (Fax)

EMC Corporation
www.emc.com
176 South Street
Hopkinton, Massachusetts 01748
508-435-1000 (Telephone)
866-464-7381 (Telephone)
617-300-6412 (Fax)

Engineous Software, Inc.
www.engineous.com
al.wojcik@engineous.com
2000 CentreGreen Way, Suite 100
Cary, North Carolina 27513
800-374-9235 (Telephone)
919-677-8911 (Fax)

Exaltec Software, Ltd.
www.exaltec.com
sales@exaltec.com
101 Federal Street, Suite 1900
Boston, Massachusetts 02110
617-342-7086 (Telephone)
617-342-7080 (Fax)

Fiorano Software, Inc.
www.fiorano.com
info@fiorano.com
718 University Avenue, Suite 212
Los Gatos, California 95032
408-354-3210 (Telephone)
800-663-3621 (Telephone)
408-354-0846 (Fax)

Forum Systems, Inc.
www.forumsystems.com
support@forumsys.com
95 Sawyer Road, Suite 110
Waltham, Massachusetts 02453
866-333-0210 (Telephone)
800-707-4590 (Telephone)

Fujitsu
www.fai.fujitsu.com
webmaster@fai.fujitsu.com
1250 East Arques Avenue

Table 8.3 (continued)   Service Technology Firms

Sunnyvale, California 94085
408-746-6200 (Telephone)
408-746-6260 (Fax)

GemStone Systems, Inc.
www.gemstone.com
sales@gemstone.com
1260 NW Waterhouse Avenue,
 Suite 200
Beaverton, Oregon 97006
503-533-3000 (Telephone)
503-533-3220 (Fax)

GigaSpaces Technologies, Inc.
www.gigaspaces.com
info@gigaspaces.com
1250 Broadway, Suite 2301
New York, New York 10001
646-421-2830 (Telephone)
646-421-2859 (Fax)

Global 360, Inc.
www.global360.com
g360.web@global360.com
2911 Turtle Creek Boulevard,
 Suite 1100
Dallas, Texas 75219
214-520-1660 (Telephone)
214-219-0476 (Fax)

GridScope, Inc.
www.gridscope.com
info@gridscope.com
San Jose, California

HandySoft Global Corporation
www.handysoft.com
1952 Gallows Road, Suite 200
Vienna, Virginia 22182
703-442-5600 (Telephone)
800-753-9343 (Telephone)
703-442-5650 (Fax)

Hewlett Packard*
www.hp.com/go/soa
19111 Pruneridge Avenue

Cupertino, California 95014
650-603-5200 (Telephone)
800-638-5231 (Telephone)

HostBridge Technology
www.hostbridge.com
info@hostbridge.com
100 East 7th Avenue
Stillwater, Oklahoma 74074
405-533-2900 (Telephone)
866-965-2427 (Telephone)

IBM Corporation*
www.ibm.com/soa
soa@us.ibm.com
Software Group
Route 100
Somers, New York 10589
1-800-IBM-4YOU

IDS Scheer North America
www.ids-scheer.com/us
info-us@ids-scheer.com
1055 WestLakes Drive, Suite 100
Berwyn, Pennsylvania 19312
610-854-6800 (Telephone)
800-810-2747 (Telephone)
610-854-7382 (Fax)

ILog, Inc.
www.ilog.com
info@ilog.com
1080 Linda Vista Avenue
Mountain View, California 94043
650-567-8000 (Telephone)
800-367-4564 (Telephone)
650-567-8001 (Fax)

Infomatica Corporation*
www.informatica.com
100 Cardinal Way
Redwood City, California 94063
650-385-5000 (Telephone)
800-653-3871 (Telephone)
650-385-5500 (Fax)

Table 8.3 (continued)   Service Technology Firms

Intalio
www.intalio.com
info@intalio.com
1000 Bridge Parkway, Suite 210
Redwood City, California 94065
650-596-1800 (Telephone)
650-596-1801 (Fax)

Integrasolv
www.integrasolv.com
info@integrasolv.com
44 Apple Street, Suite 3
Tinton Falls, New Jersey 07724
732-345-0700 (Telephone)
732-345-0777 (Fax)

Intel Corporation
www.intel.com
2200 Mission College Boulevard
Santa Clara, California 95052
408-765-8080 (Telephone)
800-538-3373 (Telephone)

Intersystems Corporation
www.intersystems.com
1 Memorial Drive
Cambridge, Massachusetts 02142-1356
617-621-0600 (Telephone)
617-494-1631 (Fax)

IONA Technologies, Inc.
www.iona.com
kim.salem@iona.com
200 West Street
Waltham, Massachusetts 02451
781-902-8888 (Telephone)
781-902-8001 (Fax)

Ipedo, Inc.
www.ipedo.com
info@ipedo.com
1001 Marshall Street
Redwood City, California 94063
650-306-4000 (Telephone)
650-306-4001 (Fax)

Itellix Software Solutions
www.itellix.com
madhukar.srivastava@itellix.com
101 Prestige Poseidon
139 Residency Road
Bangalore 560025
India
91-80-511-255-01 (Telephone)
91-80-511-255-04 (Fax)

iTKO, Inc.
www.itko.com
info@itko.com
1505 LBJ Freeway, Suite 250
Dallas, Texas 75234
877-289-4856 (Telephone)
817-281-2458 (Fax)

iWay Sify, Ltd.
www.iway.com
harleen_kaur@sifycorp.com
258 Okhla Industrial Estate
Okhla Phase 3
New Delhi 110020
India
011-510-174-39 (Telephone)
011-510-394-45 (Fax)

Jacada, Inc.
www.jacada.com
info@jacada.com
400 Perimeter Center Terrace,
 Suite 100
Atlanta, Georgia 30346
770-352-1300 (Telephone)
800-773-9574 (Telephone)
770-352-1313 (Fax)

JackBe
www.jackbe.com
4600 North Park Avenue, Suite 200
Bethesda, Maryland 20815
240-744-1274 (Telephone)

Table 8.3 (continued)   Service Technology Firms

Jitterbit, Inc.
www.jitterbit.com
info@jitterbit.com
1301 Marina Village Parkway,
 Suite 200
Alameda, California 94501
877-852-3500 (Telephone)

Jnetx
www.jnetx.com
steve.lasko@jnetx.com
7616 LBJ Freeway, Suite 720
Dallas, Texas 75251
214-597-8844 (Telephone)
972-235-9797 (Telephone)

Kabira Technologies, Inc.
www.kabira.com
info@kabira.com
1850 Gateway Drive, 5th Floor
San Mateo, California 94404
650-931-3700 (Telephone)
650-931-3799 (Fax)

**Kingdee International Software
Group**
www.kingdee.com
4/F W1-B Hi-Tech Industrial Park
Shennan Highway
Shenzhen, Peoples Republic of China
 51807

Layer 7 Technologies
www.layer7tech.com
info@layer7tech.com
700 West Georgia Street, 15th Floor
Vancouver, British Columbia V7Y 1B6
Canada
604-681-9377 (Telephone)
800-681-9377 (Telephone)
604-681-9387 (Fax)

Logic Blaze, Inc.
www.logicblaze.com
4676 Admiralty Way, Suite 520

Marina Del Rey, California 90292
310-437-4866 (Telephone)
800-822-0471 (Fax)

Lombardi Software, Inc.
www.lombardi.com
info@lombardi.com

Magic Software Enterprises, Inc.
www.magicsoftware.com
23046 Avenida de la Carlota, Suite 300
Laguna Hills, California 92653
949-250-1718 (Telephone)
800-345-6244 (Telephone)
949-250-7404 (Fax)

Majitek Pty., Ltd.
www.majitek.com
360 Elizabeth Street, Level 51
Melbourne Central Tower
Melbourne, Australia 3000
61-3-9663-8595 (Telephone)
61-3-9663-6292 (Fax)

Managed Methods
www.managedmethods.com
info@managedmethods.com
4853 Dakota Boulevard
Boulder, Colorado 80304
720-222-2694 (Telephone)
720-204-1818 (Fax)

Metastorm
www.metastorm.com
500 East Pratt Street, Suite 1250
Baltimore, Maryland 21202
443-874-1300 (Telephone)
877-321-6382 (Telephone)
443-874-1336 (Fax)

Micro Focus (IP), Ltd.
www.microfocus.com
9420 Key West Avenue
Rockville, Maryland 20850
301-838-5000 (Telephone)
301-838-5314 (Fax)

Table 8.3 (continued)   Service Technology Firms

Microsoft Corporation*
www.microsoft.com/BPM
craigsa@microsoft.com
One Microsoft Way
Redmond, Washington 98052-6399
800-642-7676 (Telephone)
425-936-7329 (Fax)

Mindreef, Inc.
www.mindreef.com
info@mindreef.com
22 Proctor Hill Road
Hollis, New Hampshire 03049
603-465-2204 (Telephone)
603-465-6583 (Fax)

Miro
www.miro.com
Waldstrasse 23
63128 Dietzenbach, Germany

MobiCents
mobicents.dev.java.net
info@mobicents.org

Novell, Inc.
www.novell.com
crc@novell.com
404 Wyman Street
Waltham, Massachusetts 02451
800-529-3400 (Telephone)
801-861-1329 (Telephone)

OpenCloud, Ltd.
www.opencloud.com
140 Cambridge Science Park
Milton Road
Cambridge CB4 0GF
United Kingdom
44-796-678-2812 (Telephone)

OpenConnect Systems, Inc.
www.openconnect.com
sales@oc.com
2711 LBJ Freeway, Suite 700
Dallas, Texas 75234

972-484-5200 (Telephone)
972-484-6100 (Fax)

OpenLink Software, Inc.
www.openlinksw.com
10 Burlington Mall Road, Suite 265
Burlington, Massachusetts 01830
781-273-0900 (Telephone)
781-229-8030 (Fax)

OpenStorm Software, Inc.
www.openstorm.com
sales@openstorm.com
4515 Seton Center Parkway,
  Suite 175
Austin, Texas 78759
713-539-8221 (Telephone)
512-236-1267 (Fax)

Oracle*
www.oracle.com/middleware
www.oracle.com/technologies/soa/
  soa-suite.html
500 Oracle Parkway
Redwood Shores, California 94065
650-506-7000 (Telephone)
800-ORACLE1 (Telephone)
650-506-7200 (Fax)

Parasoft Corporation
www.parasoft.com
info@parasoft.com
101 East Huntington Drive, 2nd Floor
Monrovia, California 91016
626-256-3680 (Telephone)
888-305-0041 (Telephone)
626-256-6884 (Fax)

Pegasystems, Inc.
www.pegasystems.com
101 Main Street
Cambridge, Massachusetts 02142-1590
617-374-9600
617-374-9620 (Fax)

Table 8.3 (continued)   Service Technology Firms

Pramati Technologies
www.pramati.com
info@pramati.com
50 Airport Parkway
San Jose, California 95110
408-435-2700 (Telephone)
408-435-2703 (Fax)

Progress Software Corporation
www.progress.com/actional
sales@actional.com
14 Oak Park
Bedford, Massachusetts 01730
650-316-3817 (Telephone)
781-280-4095 (Fax)

RatchetSoft, LLC.
www.ratchetsoft.com
sales@ratchetsoft.com
6143 Jericho Turnpike, Suite 103
Commack, New York 11725
516-620-1197 (Telephone)
516-627-6914 (Fax)

Reactivity*
www.reactivity.com
sales@reactivity.com
One Lagoon Drive, Suite 400
Redwood City, California 94065
650-551-7873 (Telephone)
650-551-7801 (Fax)

**ReadiMinds Systems and Services
Pte, Ltd.**
www.readiminds.com
3 Philip Street
18-00 Commerce Point
Singapore 048693
65-6333-1217 (Telephone)
65-6333-1719 (Fax)

Real-Time Innovations (RTI)
www.rti.com
info@rti.com
3975 Freedom Circle

Santa Clara, California 95054
408-200-4700 (Telephone)
408-200-4701 (Fax)

Rearden Commerce, Inc.
www.reardencommerce.com
1400 Fashion Island Boulevard,
 Suite 150
San Mateo, California 94404
650-212-8400 (Telephone)
877-778-2763 (Telephone)
650-212-8499 (Fax)

Recursa Software
www.recursa.com/
Van Rensselaerstraat 29-2
1058 XR Amsterdam, Netherlands
31-20-6239651 (Telephone)
31-20-7738225 (Fax)

Recursion Software, Inc.
www.recursionsw.com
info@recursionsw.com
2591 North Dallas Parkway,
 Suite 2200
Frisco, Texas 75034
972-731-8800 (Telephone)

Red Hat, Inc.*
www.redhat.com
1801 Varsity Drive
Raleigh, North Carolina 27606
919-754-3700 (Telephone)
888-REDHAT-1 (Telephone)
919-754-3701 (Fax)

Relativity Technologies, Inc.
www.relativity.com
info@relativity.com
2300 Rexwoods Drive, Suite 100
Raleigh, North Carolina 27607
919-786-2800 (Telephone)
919-786-2850 (Fax)

Rogue Wave Software, Inc.
www.roguewavesoftware.com

Table 8.3 (continued)   Service Technology Firms

Safelayer
www.safelayer.com
sflyr@safelayer.com
34-93-508-80-90

SAP America, Inc.
www.sap.com
3999 West Chester Pike
Newtown Square, Pennsylvania 19073
610-661-1000 (Telephone)
800-872-1727 (Telephone)

Savvion
www.savvion.com
5104 Old Ironsides Drive, Suite 205
Santa Clara, California 95054
408-330-3400 (Telephone)
888-544-5511 (Telephone)

Scientio, LLC.
www.scientio.com
eusales@scientio.com
Haydon House
Station Road
Woburn Sands, Bucks MK17 8RX
United Kingdom
44-1908-766151 (Telephone)
44-1908-766193 (Fax)

Seagull Software Systems, Inc.
www.seagullsoftware.com
info@seagullsoftware.com
3340 Peachtree Road NE, Suite 900
Atlanta, Georgia 30326
404-760-1560 (Telephone)
404-760-0061 (Fax)

Seapine Software, Inc.
www.seapine.com
sales@seapine.com
5412 Courseview Drive, Suite 200
Mason, Ohio 45040
513-754-1655 (Telephone)
888-683-6456 (Telephone)
513-754-1660 (Fax)

Select Business Solutions
www.selectbusinesssolutions.com
35 Nutmeg Drive
Trumbull, Connecticut 06611
888-472-7347 (Telephone)
203-383-4601 (Fax)

Servoy, Inc.
www.servoy.com
info@servoy.com
299 West Hillcrest Drive, Suite 115
Thousand Oaks, California 91360
805-624-4959 (Telephone)
805-624-4958 (Fax)

Singularity
www.singularity.co.uk/
11 Penn Plaza, 5th Floor
New York, New York 10001
212-946-2685 (Telephone)
212-946-2808 (Fax)

Skelta Software
www.skelta.com
sales@skelta.com
703-229-6732 (Telephone)
91-80-2552-0371 (Fax)

SOA Software, Inc.*
www.soa.com
info@soa.com
12100 Wilshire Boulevard, Suite 1800
Los Angeles, California 90025
310-826-1317 (Telephone)
866-SOA-9876 (Telephone)
310-820-8601 (Fax)

Software AG (Web Methods)
www.softwareag.com
webinfo@softwareag.com
Uhlandstr 12
D-64297 Darmstadt Germany
49-6151-92-0 (Telephone)
49-6151-92-1191 (Fax)

Table 8.3 (continued)   Service Technology Firms

Solstice Software, Inc.
www.solsticesoftware.com
sales@solsticesoftware.com
650 Naamans Road, Suite 207
Claymont, Delaware 19703

Sonic Software Corporation
www.sonicsoftware.com
14 Oak Park
Bedford, Massachusetts 01730
781-999-7000 (Telephone)
866-GET-SONIC (Telephone)
408-212-2720 (Fax)

SourceCode Technology Holdings, Inc.
www.k2workflow.com
4042 148th Avenue NE
Redmond, Washington 98052
8778CALLK2 (Telephone)
425-671-0411 (Fax)

StrikeIron, Inc.
www.strikeiron.com
info@strikeiron.com
2520 Meridian Parkway, Suite 150
Durham, North Carolina 27713
919-405-7010 (Telephone)
919-405-7025 (Fax)

Sun Microsystems, Inc.*
www.sun.com
4150 Network Circle
Santa Clara, California 95054
800-555-9SUN (Telephone)

Symantec Corporation
www.symantec.com
20330 Stevens Creek Boulevard
Cupertino, California 95014
408-517-8000 (Telephone)

Synergy Financial Systems
www.synergy-fs.com
info@synergy-fs.com
Synergy House

Highfields Science Park
University Boulevard
Nottingham NG7 44
United Kingdom
0 115 967 7990 (Telephone)
44 0 115 967 7933 (Fax)

Tarari, Inc.
www.tarari.com
john@tarari.com
10908 Technology Place
San Diego, California 92127
858-385-5131 (Telephone)
858-385-5129 (Fax)

Telelogic North America, Inc.
www.telelogic.com
info@telelogic.com
9401 Jeronimo Road
Irvine, California 92618
949-830-8022 (Telephone)
949-830-8023 (Fax)

Tibco Software, Inc.*
www.tibco.com
3303 Hillview Avenue
Palo Alto, California 94304
650-846-1000 (Telephone)
800-420-8450 (Telephone)
650-846-1005 (Fax)

Ultimus
www.ultimus.com
info@ultimus.com
15200 Weston Parkway, Suite 106
Cary, North Carolina 27513
919-678-0900 (Telephone)
919-678-0901 (Fax)

Verari Systems
www.verari.com
9449 Carroll Park Drive
San Diego, California 92121
858-874-3800 (Telephone)
888-942-3800 (Telephone)
858-874-3838 (Fax)

Table 8.3 (continued)   Service Technology Firms

Vitria Technology, Inc.
www.vitria.com
npatil@vitria.com
945 Stewart Drive
Sunnyvale, California 94085
408-212-2700 (Telephone)
408-212-2720 (Fax)

Vordel, Ltd.
www.vordel.com
sales@vordel.com
101 Federal Street, Suite 1900 #43
Boston, Massachusetts 02110
617-848-0974 (Telephone)
353-1-603-1701 (Fax)

WebCollage USA
www.webcollage.com
462 Seventh Avenue, 9th Floor
New York, New York 10018
212-563-2112 (Telephone)
800-616-1136 (Telephone)
212-563-2115 (Fax)

WebLayers, Inc.
www.WebLayers.com
125 Cambridge Park Drive, 6th Floor
Cambridge, Massachusetts 02142
617-500-2282 (Telephone)
617-507-8003 (Fax)

webMethods (Infravio)
www.webmethods.com
www.soamasterclass.com
miko@webmethods.com
3877 Fairfax Ridge Road, South Tower
Fairfax, Virginia 22030
703-460-2500 (Telephone)
703-460-2599 (Fax)

WebV2, Inc.
www.siemens.com
Siemens AG
Wittelsbacherplatz 2
D80333 Munich Germany
49-69-797-6660 (Telephone)

WestGlobal
www.westglobal.com
9 Exchange Place
IFSC
Dublin Ireland D1
353-1-6115100 (Telephone)

XAware, Inc.
www.xaware.com
5555 Tech Center Drive, Suite 200
Colorado Springs, Colorado 80919
719-884-5400 (Telephone)
719-884-5492 (Fax)

Xcalia USA
www.xcalia.com
745 Emerson Street
Palo Alto, California 94301
408-404-5566 (Telephone)
33-0-1-5656-1251 (Fax)

Zend Technologies, Ltd.
www.zend.com
19200 Stevens Creek Boulevard,
Suite 100
Cupertino, California 95014
888-747-9363 (Telephone)
408-253-8801 (Fax)

---

[*] Firms cited as enabling projects of SOA in multiple or single case studies of book.

Sources on SOA Standards, Technologies, and Tools

These sources on the state of SOA technology may be helpful to readers.

Publication Sources on SOA Technologies and Tools

■ *Align Journal*
Business Integration Journal (BIJ) Weekly Web Flash
www.alignjournal.com
www.bijonline.com
business_integration_journal@t2mr3.com
info@bijonline.com

■ *Business Process Trends* (*BPTrends*)
www.bptrends.com

■ *CIO*
www.cio.com

■ *CIO Insight*
www.cioinsight.com

■ *Computerworld*
www.computerworld.com

■ *Dr. Dobb's Journal*
Dr. Dobb's Enterprise SOA e-Zine
ddj@promos.sdmediagroup.com

■ *e-Week*
www.eweek.com
e-Week e-Zine
webservices@enews.eweek.com

■ *Information Week*
www.informationweek.com

■ *Infoworld*
www.infoworld.com
www.infoworld.com/3839 (Current News on SOA and SOA Product Reviews)
www.infoworld.com/3852 (Discussion on SOA Issues)
www.infoworld.com/4089 (Discussion with Experts and Technology Firms on SOA)
soareport@newsletter.infoworld.com (News on SOA)
websvcsreport@newsletter.infoworld.com (News on SOA)

- *SD Times*
  www.sdtimes.com
  info@bizmedia.com

- *SOA & BPM Times*
  www.bpm.com
  www.soa-world.com

Research Sources on SOA Technologies and Tools

- www.blogs.zdnet.com/service-oriented/?=209 (Web log on SOA)
- www.looselycoupled.com (On-demand Web services)
- www.searchwebservices.com (SOA resources)
- www.webbuyersguide.com (SOA products and services)

Sources on SOA Standards

- Association for Cooperative Operations Research and Development (ACORD)
  www.acord.org

- Business Process Management Initiative (BPMI)
  www.bpmi.org

- Financial Services Technology Consortium (FSTC)
  www.fstc.org

- Interactive Financial Exchange (IFX)
  www.ifixforum.org

- Internet Engineering Task Force (IETF)
  www.ietf.org

- Java Community Process (JCP)
  www.jcp.org

- Liberty Alliance
  www.projectliberty.org

- Object Management Group (OMG)
  www.omg.org

- Organization for the Advancement of Structured Information Standards (OASIS)
  www.oasis-open.org

- United Nations Center for Trade Facilitation and Electronic Business (UN/CEFACT)
  www.unece.org/cefact/

- Web Services Interoperability (WS-I)
  www.ws-i.org

- World Wide Web Consortium (W3C)
  www.w3c.org

Other Sources on SOA

- Association of Business Process Management Professionals
  www.abpmp.org

- Business Process Management (BPM) Conference
  www.sharedinsights.com/bpm
  customerservice@sharedinsights.com

- Enterprise Architect Summit
  www.ftponline.com/conferences/eas

- Gartner Application Integration & Web Services Summit
  www.gartner.com

- Infoworld Executive Forum Programs
  www.SOAExecForum.com

- Integration Consortium

- Global Integration Summit
  www.integrationconsortium.org

- Wall Street Technology Association
  www.wsta.org
  betsy.perkins@wsta.org

- Web Services / SOA on Wall Street Conferences and Shows
  flaggmgmt@msn.com

- Workflow Management Coalition (WfMC)
  www.wfmc.org

These sources on SOA standards, technologies, and tools complement books on the in-depth technology of Web services and SOA, such as those by Bieberstein et al., Erl, Krafzig et al., and Newcomer and Lomow, which are referenced in the Notes at the end of Chapter 1 and Chapter 9.

We conclude the section on technology in Chapter 9.

Chapter 9

Conclusion

From the results of our studies, we believe that business managers and SOA program and project staff can benefit from our emphasis on the business dimensions of SOA. Information on the technology firms (vendors), technologies, and tools in Chapter 8 can be essential but is not as important as business fundamentals. We conclude this section on technology with considerations that can guide staff who are extending or initiating projects of SOA.

Challenge of SOA and SOA Technology

The challenge of service-oriented architecture (SOA) is change, and change is difficult in a business firm. Change management can be the difference between program success and program failure, even if the business strategy and technology strategy are otherwise sound.

Collaboration of the information technology department with business departments on business process improvement projects and requirements is critical to SOA, a lesson learned in Chapters 3, 4, and 5 but collaboration of business departments with other business departments and business units, on requirements which are frequently enterprise requirements, is also critical to SOA. Collaboration on process improvement requirements if not SOA may not be effective enough in firms, thus contributing to the technology department becoming *the* expert on changing processes that are inherently business oriented not technical.[1] This difficulty can cloud delineation of core enterprise goals and processes and deployed services, and current and future requirements and determination of technologies, in a competitive continuous improvement strategy or a competitive differentiation strategy.

Although the chief executive officer (CEO) or the chief operating officer (COO) may champion, fund, and sponsor the technology department, they may be fatigued by SOA and technology[2] and defer to the chief information officer (CIO) on improving departmental or business unit processes with SOA technology, but not on improving enterprise processes in an SOA strategy.

Chief Information Officer (CIO) and SOA Technology

The CIO can be *the* champion of business processes in SOA technology that are organizationally funded and sponsored by the COO or CEO.

The criticality of the championship lies in the improvement of business enterprise processes of the firm with an SOA business strategy and SOA technology. Although a CEO or COO, an executive or a manager in a business unit, or a chief architect or an application manager in the technology department might be the champion of SOA, the CIO, as one experienced in technology and generally experienced in business, is the one who can effectively envision if not evangelize services and SOA as an enterprise strategy. Having the sponsorship of the CEO or COO, the CIO can best integrate the business experts in the business units of the firm into the strategy.

Enterprise governance of services based on strategic planning and initiated by the CIO in cooperation with the business units of the firm can ensure reusability of services in an SOA. To do this, the CIO must be a key player in business strategy. To be a key player, the CIO cannot be perceived as a pure technologist, as that contributes to the perception of the technology department and the CIO as neither a strategic function nor a strategic player or partner in the firm.[3] The CIO who can contribute to business strategy is one who can continue educating and engaging proactively the sponsors in the executive suite and those in the business units[4] on the importance of SOA and the impact of new SOA technologies. This CIO can be a leader[5] in the improvement of enterprise processes and instrumental in competitive strategy.

Criticality of Methodology and Strategy in SOA

The criticality of a disciplined but flexible program management methodology on SOA is clear in the *post facto* application of our methodology in the firms in the selected studies, as in our previous study of Web services.[6] Firms in the studies could not be constrained by formal methodological procedures. Frameworks of governance, communications, product realization, project management, architecture, data management, service management, human resource management, and post implementation can be customized by program and project staff in evolving functionality for projects of SOA.

Evolution of functionality on incremental projects of SOA contributing immediate benefits can be a prudent SOA strategy, and focus on service standards at the beginning of programs and projects of SOA can help in the foundation of an SOA strategy, lessons learned in previous chapters.

Integration of partnered platform technology firms knowledgeable in the business processes of the business firm and in open standards and technologies of SOA can also be, and continues to be, helpful in an evolutionary implementation of projects of SOA. SOA as an evolutionary and flexible strategy is evident in the bulk of the firms in the studies.

Education in a Learning Organization of SOA

Emphasis on education of staff continues to be critical in SOA strategy.

Focus on service orientation training of technical staff and business staff and continuous technical training of technical staff are crucial for implementation of an SOA strategy.

For technical staff, substantial training in business process and firm and industry strategy is as important as — if not more important than — technology training, so that this staff can optimize processes with SOA technology.[7] Knowledge transfer of technologies and tools of the technology firms to the internal technical staff is also important in the management of the SOA program and of technology firms. Training is critical from the beginning of service programs, so that the technical staff and the business staff become cognizant of the evolution and the implications of the SOA strategy. Training may include integration of SOA centers of excellence and communities of practice of technical and business staff, and councils of expertise of the technical staff,[8] for improving synchronization of technology strategy with business strategy. This is an example of a continuous learning organization.

Integration of participants from consulting firms or technology firms can be helpful in the implementation of initial training if they are properly managed by the SOA program staff.

Education and training is crucial in any SOA strategy.

Future Proposition of SOA

Finally, SOA is a feasibly strong proposition for a business firm.

Firms that hesitate to invest adequately in an SOA program may be hindered by not having competitive processes that might furnish an improved proposition of service to their customers and trusted partners. Managers might evaluate processes in their firms for future competitive advantage in their proposition and focus investment in SOA technology toward those processes.

[Firms] that anticipate the power of information technology will be in control of events. [Firms] that do not respond will be forced to accept changes that [other firms] initiate and will find themselves at a competitive disadvantage.[9]

Managers and staff in business firms initiating a competitive differentiation strategy will likely take advantage of new technologies and tools of the SOA technology firms. They will transform their own firms with technology and with urgency and a vision specific toward their organizations.[10]

This transformation will be an evolutionary and progressive SOA strategy transforming the organizations toward an SOE when combined with our program management methodology or other similar methodologies.

Because of the continued commotion and hype on service technology, our considerations of the challenge of SOA, the CIO and SOA technology, the criticality of methodology and strategy, the education and training of staff, and the future proposition of SOA provide guidance for the extension or initiation of projects of SOA. Together with our recommended program management methodology and the results of our studies, they are essentially a snapshot of SOA today that can be helpful to both program and project staff. These considerations convey our belief that the excitement of SOA technology must be balanced with the prudence of SOA business strategy.

We are confident that our message will be evident in substantive and successful SOA strategies!

We conclude the technology section with a chapter on service terminology, which is the final chapter of the book.

Notes

1. Alter, A. 2006. Pushing for a Process Edge: Lack of Cross-Functional Cooperation Thwarts BPI. *CIO Insight*, October, p. 55.
2. Harris, J. and Nichols, D. 2006. The Business Case for SOA. *Optimize*, December, p. 72.
3. Alter, A. 2006. Top 30 Trends for 2007: CIOs Strive to Be Strategic. *CIO Insight*, December, p. 26.
4. Smith, G.S. 2006. *Straight to the Top: Becoming a World-Class CIO*. John Wiley & Sons, Inc., Hoboken, NJ, p. 84, 86, 226.
5. Hugos, M. 2006. Ticktock, Ticktock. *CIO*, November 15, p. 38.
6. Anderson, D., Howell-Barber, H., Hill, J., Javed, N., Lawler, J., and Li, Z. 2005. A Study of Web Services Projects in the Financial Services Industry. *Information Systems Management*, Winter, p. 75.
7. Alter, Top 30 Trends for 2007: CIOs Struggle to Find Business-Savvy Technologists. *CIO Insight*, December, p. 33.
8. Alter, A. 2006. SOA Success: Five Actions CIOs Say You Should Take — Coordinate IT and the Business. *CIO Insight*, November 14, p. 1–2.
9. Porter, M. 1998. *On Competition*. Harvard Business School Press, Boston, MA, p. 98.
10. Kotter, J.P. 2007. Leading Change: Why Transformation Efforts Fail. *Harvard Business Review*, January, p. 97–100.

Chapter 10

Service Terminology

Agile methodology: Flexible and iterative techniques enabling rapid incremental deliverables.

Agility, efficiency, and flexibility benefits: Business factor for extent to which benefits of adjusting to business environments drive the program.

Analysis: Initial phase of product realization framework of program management methodology.

Application developer: Technology participant who develops user interfaces to services based on business rules and executes unit testing.

Application integration and legacy adaptation tools: Tools enabling legacy components as services in an SOA.

Application project manager: Technology participant who manages application project requirements and schedules to ensure product realization of SOA.

Architecture: Framework in program management methodology enabling compliance of business processes with an SOA model.

Asset inventory management tools: Tools for managing hardware and software technologies in an SOA.

Asset librarian: Governance participant who furnishes cross-reference of applications, data, programs, processes, and services on SOA, and maintains a catalog for the firm.

Asset management: Approach for controlling the life cycle of hardware and software technologies in an SOA.

Association for Cooperative Operations Research and Development (ACORD): Organization for defining service standards in the insurance industry.

Asynchronous Service Access Protocol (ASAP): Standard for management of services.

Behaved data services: Data services that do not disrupt applications of the firm.

Best-of-class tools: Technical factor for extent to which specialty tools from pure-play or third-party technology firms are included on the program.

Block Extensible Exchange Protocol (BEEP): Standard for exchange of interactions.

Business analyst: Business participant who defines and formalizes business process and service requirements of SOA in internal business departments and business units of the firm.

Business analyst for extended organization: Business participant who defines and formalizes business process and service requirements of SOA with external business units or partnered firms.

Business client: Business participant who defines business process and service requirements and is an eventual consumer of business processes and services.

Business client participation: Business factor for the extent to which business departments consent, contribute, and furnish content and guidance to the program.

Business compliance specialist: Governance participant who maintains documentation of government and industry legal and regulatory requirements and audits compliance.

Business documentalist: Business participant who documents existing and future business processes and services of SOA.

Business domain: Collection of business processes containing loosely coupled services.

Business enterprise architecture: Definition of business processes, business policies, and information technology (IT) infrastructure, based on a definition of what the firm does as a business.

Business manager: Business participant who manages business project requirements and schedules in liaison with application project manager to ensure SOA product realization.

Business operations sponsor: Business participant who approves and funds product realization for projects of SOA requested by business operations organizations.

Business process: Set of logically related tasks designed to achieve defined business outcomes.

Business process coordinator: Business participant who ensures collective focus on improvement of processes on projects of SOA and helps in the deployment of services.

Business process management (BPM): Approach for achieving business goals, coordinating end-to-end processes of the firm, establishing best practices, and furnishing software.

Business process management and modeling tools: Tools for analyzing processes of the firm.

Business Process Management Initiative (BPMI): Organization for defining process standards.

Business process management software: Technical factor for extent to which Web Services-Business Process Execution Language (WS-BPEL) software is included in the program.

Business process management system (BPMS): Software for graphical process modeling, testing, implementation, and monitoring.

Business Process Modeling Language (BPML): Meta-language for interaction of services.

Business process modeling notation (BPMN): Graphical notation of processes of workflows.

Business Process Query Language (BPQL): Standardized language for interface with a business process management system (BPMS).

Business process project specialist: Business participant who ensures process and service projects are initiated in conformance with SOA business strategy.

Business process specialist: Business participant who applies advanced knowledge of business process management and tools to design, model, test, and implement processes.

Business sponsor: Business participant who approves and funds product realization of projects of SOA requested by business units.

Business support coordinator: Business participant who empowers business consumer staff in constructive service usage.

Business testing coordinator: Business participant who coordinates testing of SOA between business staff and technical staff.

Business testing specialist: Business participant who develops and executes testing plans and scripts to validate data, interfaces, and business rules.

Business visionary: Business participant who envisions full potential of SOA as a business proposition and articulates business requirements in an SOA strategy.

Change management: Procedural factor for extent to which procedures are evident for ensuring optimal resolution of requests for changes in existing processes or services or of requests for new processes or services.

Chief information officer (CIO): Senior manager of information technology department and often champion of SOA.

Choreography: Definition of conditions and sequences by which messages are exchanged between or in business processes.

Collaboration facilitator: Governance participant who facilitates constructive and close collaboration of business staff and technical staff on projects of SOA.

Common reference: Procedural factor for extent to which business and technical terminology is applied consistently by program staff.

Communications: Framework in program management methodology enabling emphasis on business criticality of SOA in the firm.

Communications coordinator: Governance participant who coordinates evangelization of the SOA program and SOA strategy and defines common terminology for program staff.

Competitive, market and regulatory differentials: Business factor for extent to which competitive, market, and regulatory first-mover edge for the firm drives the program.

Competitive differentiation strategy: Strategy of exceeding equivalency with competitor firms for an extended and longer duration.

Competitive equivalency strategy: Strategy of equivalency in core services with competitor firms.

Component services: Discrete services within a process.

Composite services: A number of discrete services combined into performing a process.

Configuration and deployment management tools: Tools for ensuring effective deployment of processes and services.

Consumer: Business or technical clients that access services.

Continuous process improvement: Procedural factor for extent to which procedures are evident for iterative improvement of existing and new processes.

Continuous improvement strategy: Strategy of exceeding equivalency with competitor firms for a defined but shorter duration than competitive differentiation strategy.

Control of program: Procedural factor for extent to which a formal function is evident for guiding and helping the firm in evolution to SOA.

Costing techniques: Procedural factor for extent to which techniques are evident for costing existing and future SOA product realization and support.

Customer demand: Business factor for extent to which customer demand for enhanced service from technology drives the program.

Culture of innovation: Business factor for extent to which innovation in business and technical practices is encouraged and facilitates the program.

Database administrator: Technology participant who converts logical database design into physical databases and maintains databases.

Database analyst: Technology participant who models logical data requirements and maintains data catalogs and schema catalogs.

Database developer: Technology participant who creates data services with SQL or eXtensible Markup Language (XML).

Data management: Framework in program management methodology enabling behaved SOA data services that do not disrupt applications of the firm.

Data management and transformation tools: Tools for manipulating data and transforming data to and from eXtensible Markup Language (XML).

Data model: Graphical description of the design of a database.

Data tools: Technical factor for extent to which data tools supporting eXtensible Markup Language (XML) are included on the program.

Design: Phase in product realization framework of program management methodology in which technology for a business solution is proposed by the technology department.

Deployment and implementation: Final phase of product realization framework of program management methodology.

Deployment specialist: Technology participant who does rollout of services and ensures education and training of business staff and technical staff on usage of services.

Development: Phase of product realization framework of program management methodology.

Development, integration, and service tools: Tools for creating and establishing relationships between service components.

Education and training: Procedural factor for extent to which formal skill training on services and SOA is evident for program staff.

Electronic Business eXtensible Markup Language (ebXML): Standardized language for modeling processes.

Enterprise application integration (EAI): Middleware for integrating data or functionality from diverse applications.

Enterprise architect: Governance participant who helps project staff on design of infrastructure, design of services, and reusability of services in an evolutionary SOA strategy.

Enterprise architecture: Business factor for the extent to which formal enterprise architecture contributes to initiation of the program and evolves with processes to an SOA.

Enterprise service bus (ESB): Messaging layer for services.

Executive business leadership: Business factor for the extent to which senior managers in the business units evangelize business criticality of SOA as a strategy.

Executive sponsor: Corporate participant who advocates SOA as a program and a strategy, and funds governance of SOA as a *bona fide* function in the firm.

Executive sponsorship: Business factor for extent to which senior managers in the firm articulate and evangelize business criticality of SOA as a strategy and fund the program.

Executive technology leadership: Business factor for the extent to which senior managers in the technology departments evangelize the technical and business criticality of SOA as a strategy.

eXtensible Markup Language (XML): Standardized language for creating client-defined tags for data elements and content of messages.

eXtensible Markup Language (XML) Encryption: Standard for protecting confidentiality of a message.

eXtensible Markup Language (XML) Signature: Standard for ensuring the content of a message.

eXtensible Markup Language (XML) standard: Technical factor for extent to which XML is included in the program.

External process domain on project: Technical factor for the extent to which external tightly coupled and security-sensitive and trusted projects contribute to the evolution of SOA.

External SOA domain on project: Technical factor for the extent to which external standards compliant, loosely coupled, and security sensitive and trusted projects contribute to the evolution of SOA.

File Transfer Protocol (FTP): Standard for exchange of files.

Finance planner: Governance participant who controls program budget on projects of SOA and costing techniques on service level agreements (SLAs) between technology departments and business units.

Financial benefits: Business factor for the extent to which benefits of increased revenues or decreased expenses drive the program.

Financial Services Technology Consortium: Organization for defining service standards in the financial industry.

Focus on improvement of process: Business factor for the extent to which improvement of business processes, process integration, and service choreography are the goals of the program.

Framework: Group of coupled or related tasks for managing a program or a project of SOA.

Governance: Framework in program management methodology ensuring alignment of processes and services with business strategy and resulting in evolution to a service-oriented enterprise (SOE).

Gramm-Leach-Bliley Financial Services Modernization Act: Regulatory requirements often driving implementation of SOA in the financial industry.

Granularity: Modularity of a service.

Health Insurance Portability and Accountability Act (HIPAA): Regulatory requirements often driving implementation of SOA in the health industry.

Help desk: Technology participant who helps technical and business staff in problem resolution on the usage of services in SOA.

Human resource management: Framework in program management methodology enabling identification of new and revised responsibilities and roles of business and technical staff on SOA.

Hypertext Transfer Protocol (HTTP): Standard for interaction with servers on the Web.

Information management: Procedural factor for extent to which procedures are evident for ensuring data integrity and quality for technical and business functions.

Infrastructure architect: Technology participant who advises project staff on infrastructure, collaborates with the enterprise architect, and maintains infrastructure for the firm.

Infrastructure architecture: Procedural factor for extent to which procedures are evident for guiding the evolution of technology in a strategy of SOA.

Infrastructure availability administrator: Technology participant who maintains and monitors capacity, scalability, and performance of SOA infrastructure.

Infrastructure project manager: Technology participant who manages infrastructure project requirements and schedules to ensure realization of SOA.

Infrastructure tool expert: Technology participant who builds complicated components of infrastructure for composite service usage by project technical staff.

Integration specialist: Technology participant who merges components of services for testing and deployment.

Integration and testing: Phase of product realization framework of program management methodology.

Interactive Financial Exchange (IFX) Organization: Organization for defining service standards in the financial industry.

Internal process domain on project: Technical factor for extent to which complex Web services applications contribute to the evolution of SOA.

Internal SOA domain on project: Technical factor for the extent to which standards compliant, internal, and loosely coupled projects contribute to the evolution of SOA.

Internal Web services on project: Technical factor for the extent to which Web services as simple projects contribute to the evolution of SOA.

Internet Engineering Task Force (IETF): Organization for defining Internet specifications.

Java Application Program Interface (API) for eXtensible Markup Language (XML) Remote Procedure Call (JAX-RPC): Standard for extraction and mapping of Simple Object Access Protocol (SOAP) mechanisms.

Java Community Process (JCP) Organization: Organization for defining Java specifications and standards.

Knowledge coordinator: Governance participant who coordinates and ensures infusion of knowledge of service orientation to business staff and technical staff on projects of SOA.

Knowledge exchange: Procedural factor for the extent to which processes and procedures are evident for informing business and technical staff of the progress of the program.

Knowledge management tools: Tools for transforming information into knowledge.

Legacy adapter developer: Technology participant who converts the legacy components of services.

Legacy application: Existing applications requiring new functionality.

Liberty Alliance: Organization for defining service security standards.

Loosely coupled: Services linked with other services only at runtime.

Management and monitoring tools: Tools for monitoring the performance of services in an SOA.

Message Transmission Optimization Mechanism (MTOM): Standard for optimization of Simple Object Access Protocol (SOAP) message transmission.

Messaging standards: Technical factor for the extent to which technology supporting Simple Object Access Protocol (SOAP), SOAP Message Transmission Optimization Mechanism (MTOM), and SOAP with Attachments (SwA) or similar standards is included in the program.

Methodology for Enabling Service-Oriented Architecture (MESOA): Program management methodology of non-agile and agile project management techniques and methodology in this book.

Middleware: Software for performing conversion, translation, consolidation, and integration on behalf of business applications.

Middleware: Technical factor for the extent to which an enterprise service bus (ESB) or traditional middleware technology is included in the program.

Middleware and service bus tools: Tools for integrating data and functionality from diverse application sources.

Naming conventions: Procedural factor for the extent to which naming standards and service versioning are used by program staff.

Networking tools: Tools for managing and monitoring a network.

Non-agile methodology: Non-flexible and sequential "waterfall" development of applications.

Object Management Group (OMG) Organization: Organization for defining standards in object-oriented programming and system modeling.

On-demand services: Final evolution of SOA to a service-oriented enterprise (SOE) in which services are delivered as needed to consumers.

Orchestration: Definition of rules for flow of services in a process.

Organization for the Advancement of Structured Information Standards (OASIS): Organization for defining interoperability between Web services core standards.

Organizational change management: Business factor for the extent to which cultural change management is evident in helping business and technical staff embrace the program.

Personnel specialist: Corporate participant who supports SOA by identifying organizational obstacles on projects of SOA and initiating remedial solutions.

Platform of key technology firms: Technical factor for the extent to which the platforms from key technology firms are included in the program.

Platform specialty tools from platform technology firm: Technical factor for the extent to which specialty tools of the platform technology firms are included in the program.

Portal: Gateway to multiple internal or external partnered firm applications.

Portlet: Small application functioning in a portal.

Post implementation: Framework in program management methodology enabling service and process life-cycle tasks following product realization.

Process and service deployment environment: Procedural factor for the extent to which procedures are evident for furnishing software and tools to the development staff in the program.

Process and service deployment techniques: Procedural factor for the extent to which procedures are evident to ensure the highest quality of deployed technology throughout the program.

Process specialist: Governance participant who models business and technical processes on projects of SOA.

Procurement of technology: Procedural factor for the extent to which a formal function is evident for furnishing quality hardware and software technology to the program in a cost-effective and expeditious manner.

Procurement specialist: Governance participant who enables procurement of required SOA technologies from technology firms in a cost-effective and expeditious manner.

Product realization: Framework in program management methodology enabling analysis and design, development, integration and testing, and deployment and implementation of SOA, and is the core of established project management methodology.

Program methodology specialist: Governance participant who adjusts product delivery procedures and processes to ensure a balance of control and flexibility.

Project management: Framework in program management methodology enabling delivery of projects of SOA.

Project planner: Governance participant who advises project managers on project planning of SOA and adjustments, and maintains an archive of best practices and worst practices.

Proprietary technologies: Technical factor for the extent to which proprietary software is included in the program.

Provider: Publisher of services in the firm.

Reference architecture: Blueprint of proposed architecture in technical terminology.

Registry: Database of information on available services, but not the services themselves.

Registry and repository tools: Tools for maintaining inventory of services and associations.

Repository: Database of information on available services.

Representational State Transfer (REST): An alternative to, if not a simplification of, the Simple Object Access Protocol (SOAP) and Web services.

Responsibilities and roles: Procedural factor for the extent to which the responsibilities and roles of staff in the program are clearly defined for completing project tasks.

Reusability of assets: Business factor for the extent to which multiple services using software technologies constitute a goal of the program.

Risk management: Procedural factor for the extent to which procedures are evident for mitigating failure or loss caused by SOA.

Risk specialist: Governance participant who furnishes guidelines for risk management on projects of SOA and informs project managers and staff of technical, market, human, and compliance risks.

Run time tools: Tools for monitoring the performance of applications exposed as services.

Sarbanes–Oxley Insurance Portability and Accountability Act (SOX): Regulatory requirements often driving implementation of SOA in industry.

Securities Exchange Commission (SEC) Rule 17a-4: Regulatory requirements often driving implementation of SOA in the financial securities industry.

Security Assertions Markup Language (SAML): Standard for exchange of security assertions between security domains.

Security management: Procedural factor for extent to which procedures are evident for safeguarding access to services.

Service management and support: Procedural factor for the extent to which procedures are evident for ensuring service availability and reusability and furnishing metrics on service support.

Security specialist: Technology participant who helps project staff on security techniques and technologies.

Security standards: Technical factor for extent to which technology supporting eXtensible Markup Language (XML) Encryption, XML Signature, Web Services-Federation (WS-F), Web Services-Security (WS-S), and Web Services-Security Policy (WS-SP) or similar standards is included on the program.

Service administrator: Technology participant who maintains and monitors security of services in SOA.

Service availability administrator: Technology participant who maintains and monitors availability of services in consumer business units of the firm through service metrics.

Service Description and Discovery Standards: Technical factor for the extent to which technology supporting Universal Description, Discovery and Integration (UDDI), Web Services Description Language (WSDL), and Web Services-Policy (WS-Policy) or similar standards is included in the program.

Security tools: Tools for detecting network intrusion and securing network services.

Service: Application component deployed on a network, described in a Web services description, and capable of responding to requests for services.

Service availability administrator: Technology participant who tunes architecture to support service level agreements (SLAs).

Service catalog management: Procedural factor for the extent to which procedures for managing a registry or a repository of processes and services are evident in the program.

Service contract: Agreement between a consumer and a provider of services.

Service domain owner: Technology participant who inherits deployed processes and services, and ensures continued collaboration of business staff and technical staff.

Service level agreement (SLA): Contract between a provider of services and a consumer of services defining the objectives of quality.

Service librarian: Governance participant who maintains the SOA service catalog for the firm.

Service manager: Technology participant who ensures availability of production services and schedules support tasks.

Service management: Framework in program management methodology enabling continued conformity and coordination of processes and services to the business strategy defined in framework of governance.

Service orchestration: Rules for the flow of services within a business process.

Service-oriented architecture (SOA): Enabling framework for integrating business processes and supporting information technology infrastructure as loosely coupled and secure, standardized components — services — that can be reused and combined to address changing business priorities.

Service-oriented enterprise (SOE): Full deployment of all processes of the firm as services in an "on-demand" SOA.

Service orientation: Business factor for the extent to which technical and business staff is receptive to principles of service orientation and SOA.

Service Provisioning Markup Language (SPML): Standard for allocation of resources.

Service taxonomy: Description of relationships between services.

Simple Mail Transfer Protocol (SMTP): Standard for definition of simple text messaging.

Simple Object Access Protocol (SOAP): Former description for eXtensible Markup Language (XML) protocol for exchanging messages between interacting services.

Simple Object Access Protocol (SOAP) Message Transmission Optimization Mechanism (MTOM): Standard for optimization of SOAP message transmission with attachments.

Simple Object Access Protocol (SOAP) with Attachments (SwA): Standard for appending information to SOAP messages.

SOA center of competency: Procedural factor for extent to which a centralized team is evident for furnishing SOA expertise help to program staff.

SOA developer: Technology participant who creates service metadata, defines interfaces to services, defines messaging, assembles services, and executes unit testing.

SOA program coordinator: Governance participant who coordinates alignment of projects of SOA with enterprise architecture and business strategy.

SOA strategist: Governance participant who creates SOA business strategy as an evolutionary strategy and defines a function of governance to manage an SOA program.

Software architect: Technology participant who enables analysis and design and optional prototyping of project requirements of SOA.

Standards management: Procedural factor for extent to which program staff is cognizant of official standards, scope of implementation of the standards by technology firms, and standard gap resolution techniques.

Strategic planning: Business factor for extent to which the business strategy of SOA is articulated in the firm and is accepted by program staff.

Strategy management: Procedural factor for extent to which procedures are evident for evaluating and improving program strategy of SOA as required.

System manager: Technology participant who manages hardware and software infrastructure.

Team leader: Technology participant who manages product realization tasks of project technology teams and furnishes project status to project managers.

Technical client: Technology participant who defines technical service requirements and is a consumer of technical services.

Technical documentalist: Technology participant who documents services of projects of SOA.

Technical domain: Collection of technical processes containing loosely coupled services.

Technical testing specialist: Technology participant who develops scripts to test interoperability of services and executes testing with business staff.

Technical visionary: Technology participant who envisions the potential of SOA as a business proposition and formalizes technical requirements in an SOA strategy.

Technology compliance specialist: Governance participant who maintains documentation of industry and organizational technological standards and performs audits.

Technology firm knowledge capture: Procedural factor for the extent to which program staff captures knowledge from hardware and software technology firms to be independent of the technology firms.

Technology knowledge specialist: Governance participant who helps in knowledge transfer to staff on projects of SOA.

Technical sponsor: Technology participant who funds realization of processes and services on projects of SOA.

Testing tools: Tools for ensuring service quality.

Tool administrator: Technology participant who maintains and monitors usage of specialized tools of SOA.

Training specialist: Corporate participant who maintains organizational support of SOA by implementing required training on service orientation and SOA.

Transaction standards: Technical factor for extent to which technology supporting Web Services-Composite Application Framework (WS-CAF), Web Services-Choreography Description Language (WS-CDL), and Web Services-Transaction (WS-TX), SQL Transactions, or similar standards is included in the program.

United Nations Center for Trade Facilitation and Electronic Business (UN/CEFACT): Organization for defining international service standards.

Universal Description, Discovery and Integration (UDDI): Standard for publishing services in a registry that can be discovered by applications on any computing platform.

United States of America (USA) Patriot Act: Regulatory requirements often driving implementation of SOA in industry.

User interface standards: Technical factor for extent to which user interface tools or Web Services-Remote Portlets (WS-RP) are included in the program.

Web services: Family of technologies consisting of specifications, protocols, and industry-based standards used by heterogeneous applications to communicate, collaborate, and exchange information among themselves in a secure, reliable, and interoperable manner.

Web services best practices: Technical factor for extent to which Web Services Interoperability (WS-I) is included in the program.

Web Services Atomic Transaction (WS-AT): Standard for granular transactions.

Web Services Business Process Execution Language (WS-BPEL): Standard for definition of business processes as services.

Web Services Choreography (WS-C): Standard for description of conditions and sequences of exchange of messages between services.

Web Services Choreography Description Language (WS-CDL): Standard for description of conditions and sequences of messages.

Web Services Composite Application Framework (WS-CAF): Standard for coordination of transactions.

Web Services Conversation Language (WSCL): Standard for exchange of documents.

Web Services Description Language (WSDL): eXtensible Markup Language (XML) standard for description, location, and invocation methods of services.

Web Services Distributed Management (WS-DM): Standard for control of resources for services.

Web Services Eventing (WS-E): Standard for exchange of event messaging.

Web Services Experience Language (WSXL): Standard for interactive applications.

Web Services Federation (WS-F): Standard for collaboration and single sign-on.

Web Services Flow Language (WSFL): Standard for description of processes.

Web Services Inspection Language (WSIL): Standard for discovery of services not in a Universal Description, Discovery and Integration (UDDI) registry.

Web Services Interoperability (WS-I): Standard for interoperability of services.

Web Services Interoperability (WS-I) Organization: Organization for defining interoperability between standards and technologies.

Web Services Invocation Framework (WSIF): Standard for extension of Web Services Description Language (WSDL).

Web services management standards: Technical factor for extent to which Service Provisioning Markup Language (SPML) and Web Services-Distributed Management (WS-DM) are included on the program.

Web Services Metadata Exchange (WS-Metadata Exchange): Standard for dynamic access of metadata.

Web Services Notification (WS-N): Standard for notification and publication of services.

Web Services Policy (WS-Policy): Standard for description of service specifications.

Web Services Provisioning (WS-Provisioning): Standard for description of schemas in order to enable interoperability between provisioning applications.

Web Services Reliable Messaging (WS-RM): Standard for guarantee of integrity of messages during failure of infrastructure.

Web Services Reliability (WS-R): Standard for guarantee of delivery of messaging.

Web Services Remote Portlets (WS-RP): Standard for embedding remote services into portal pages.

Web Services Resource Framework (WS-RF): Standard for access of stateful resources with Web services.

Web Services Secure Conversation (WS-SC): Standard for exchange of data in a secure session.

Web Services Security (WS-S): Standard for guarantee of service security across a firewall.

Web Services Security Policy (WS-SP): Standard for association of security policy with services.

Web Services Transaction (WS-TX): Standard for reliability of a transaction using protocols instead of shared technology.

Web Services Transaction Management (WS-TM): Standard for interaction between existing transaction managers.

Web Services Transfer (WS-Transfer): Standard for acquisition of entity representations.

Web Services Trust (WS-Trust): Standard for management of relationships of trust.

World Wide Web Consortium (W3C): Organization for standardizing Web technologies.

Index